GET OUT OF YOUR HEAD

Volume 2: Navigating the Abyss of Depression

By Brian Sachetta

For Nana

TABLE OF CONTENTS

DISCLAIMER

Many events in this book have been recreated from memory. As such, alternative versions of the stories within may exist. In addition, the author and publisher have changed or omitted several names and details in those stories to maintain the anonymity of the people and organizations involved in them.

The author and publisher have also made every attempt to verify the information in this book. However, mistakes may still be present; neither party assumes responsibility for any errors, omissions, or contrary interpretations of the content herein.

This book contains the opinions and ideas of its author. Its purpose is to provide helpful, general information on the subjects it addresses. It is not meant to be used — nor should it be used — to diagnose or treat any medical condition. For the diagnosis or treatment of any disease or ailment, readers should consult their physicians.

Lastly, the author and publisher cannot and do not guarantee any specific results from reading this book or implementing the strategies described in it. Nor will they be held liable for any injury, damage, or loss that any reader may incur as a direct or indirect consequence of following the directions or suggestions given herein. Though they stand behind this book's content and welcomingly offer it to their audience, they remind that audience that each reader is responsible for his or her actions and the outcomes associated with them.

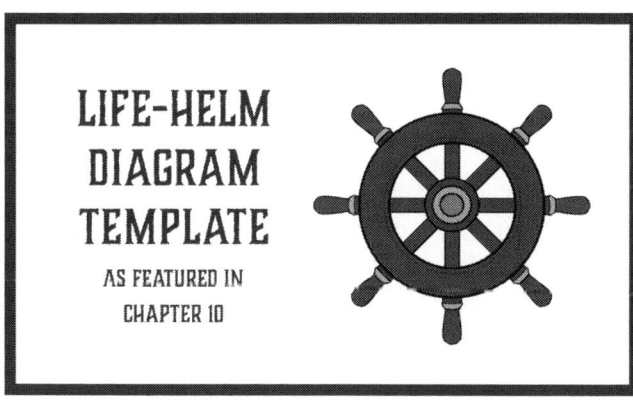

LIFE-HELM DIAGRAM TEMPLATE

AS FEATURED IN CHAPTER 10

CLAIM YOUR GIFT

Finding and maintaining balance in life is vital when it comes to managing depression. It's also really difficult. That's why I created what I call the Life-Helm Diagram.

It's a visual representation of the most important areas of our lives and our satisfaction with each of those areas.

We discuss it in full detail in chapter 10, which is why I'd like you to have a copy / template of it. It's certainly not a requirement, but it will be easier to follow along and implement the recommended exercises if you have it.

To grab your free copy today, head to:

www.getoutofyourhead.com/abyss-gift

ANOTHER JOURNEY BEGINS

Depression is a monster. It's our own personal leviathan, quietly waiting for us in the middle of the ocean. It's also an invisible illness; in merely having a conversation with someone, you'd seldom be able to tell whether he or she is dealing with the affliction. And yet, according to statistics, more than ten percent of Americans suffer from it each year, and more than twenty percent will at some point in their lives.[1]

This behemoth is also the leading cause of disability for Americans aged fifteen to forty-four.[2] That incapacitation and the treatment and workplace costs associated with it are among the main reasons the disorder impacts the US economy by more than $200 billion annually.[3] Thus, it's apparent, on many levels, this monster is both everywhere and nowhere at the same time.

Year after year, millions of dollars pour into research on the subject,[4] and more thought leaders offer their takes on the disorder, expanding the already sizable repository of content on this taboo topic. But despite that growing amount of wisdom and a five-fold increase[5] in antidepressant use in the last thirty years,[6] the disease's prevalence is still increasing at a significant rate.[7]

So, why do the numbers associated with depression keep rising, despite our efforts and good intentions? That's a complicated, difficult question, but it's one I'll attempt to answer throughout this book. If I could give an overview of that answer, however, I'd say, like the question itself, depression is a complex disease composed of many different factors. That means, to treat it in full, we need to address all of its parts — something our society doesn't currently do. Until that changes, we'll likely continue to see new cases outpace the resolution of existing ones.

If I may say so myself, two well-known psychiatrists who likely would've agreed with this take were George Engel and John Romano of the University of Rochester. In 1977, the pair proposed their *biopsychosocial model*,[8] an interdisciplinary framework for evaluating and treating diseases — one that rivaled and expanded upon the more popular, physiology-focused *biomedical model*. With it, they suggested that illnesses and mental disorders arise as a result of the complex interactions between the biological, psychological, and social aspects of our lives — not just from the body itself.

When it comes to discussing depression, though not every framework will admit it, each of these areas or "spheres" of influence matters quite a bit, as they all contribute to our experience of the disease. So, to help simplify that discussion, let's define these categories in ways we can all understand. Specifically, let's assume "biological" refers to our genetics, brains, and bodies, "psychological" encompasses our thoughts and beliefs, and "social" covers just about everything else.

Now, according to this three-pronged model, if we treat or improve any one of its spheres, we'll inevitably affect the others in some fashion as well. To give you an example of what that might look like, let's pretend we regularly experience social anxiety and are heading to a networking event tonight. Before arriving at that event, if we confront the psychological aspect of our fear by telling ourselves a new, more empowering story on how we're feeling, we'll bring ourselves relief in more ways than one.

To kick off that process, we could first reassure ourselves that our anxiety — heart palpitations and all — isn't our body's way of telling us something's wrong but a unique form of energy that helps us bring excitement to the task at hand. By thinking such comforting thoughts, we'll likely alter our brain chemistry to a degree and become more hopeful about the event in general. These uplifting feelings will then increase our odds of safely connecting with others, which, in turn, will reinforce our new story and make our anxiety slightly more manageable overall. And while I admit that alleviating difficult emotions isn't always as easy as I'm making it sound, I think the simplicity of this example illustrates the holistic nature of Engel and Romano's framework.

When it comes to leveraging that framework, however, we don't always have to start with the psychological realm. We can also first tackle one of the other sectors of our model, regardless of whether we're talking about anxiety or almost any other mental disorder. Yet, when treating depression, our society tends to put forth a different kind of message altogether. Specifically, it tells us to focus on the biological side of things — most notably via psychiatric medication. As such, we prescribe early and often, hoping our medicine will change our neurotransmitter activity, boost our mood, and, ultimately, drive us to make positive, lasting changes.

Of course, thankfully, it sometimes does just that, acting as both a key to long-term recovery and a more straightforward solution than some of the others available to us. Yet, as encouraging as those two characteristics might be, they don't necessarily indicate that a treatment plan consisting *exclusively* of medication is the best approach, either. There are a couple of reasons behind such a conclusion. The first is that medication is just one possible way of addressing the biological realm of our model; we can also utilize workout regimens, depression-related eating plans,[9] and power poses.[10]

The second is that when we focus on any one part of that model, we're subconsciously assuming it works in a *bottom-up* fashion. By bottom-up, I mean we suppose it has a designated start and end point and that when we send help to its origin, it propagates up to the remaining parts in a straight-line fashion.

Though these presumptions aren't totally inaccurate, they do ignore a large piece of the puzzle. Specifically, while something like medication can absolutely be a catalyst for change, an approach based solely on it disregards the fact that the biopsychosocial model isn't a one-way street but an interwoven system of bidirectional roads. In other words, each aspect of that model influences the remaining two, no matter which one we start with. And that means, if we focus on one in particular and overlook the others, we miss out on a whole host of interactions between the spheres that could further improve our well-being.

Don't get me wrong, though. This isn't an attack on psychotropic drugs. It's just a warning against focusing on any *one* of the spheres in our model. Though medication certainly isn't for everyone, it's unquestionably helpful for some and life-saving for others. Dismissing it, or any other part of the biological sphere, for that matter, would be just as ignorant of me as disregarding the psychological or social influences on depression.

One other thing I think this model tells us is why we haven't yet found a *magic cure* for the condition. We all have different wants and needs in our biological, psychological, and social worlds. Moreover, each of us responds differently to various changes in those worlds. Discovering a cure then, if that's what we want to call it, would mean finding something that balances all of our desires across all three of those spheres. That's a tall order.

Instead of looking for that elusive cure-all, throughout this book, we'll investigate all three parts of the model and how they interact with one another to ultimately create the experiences we know as mental health and illness. Since I'm not a doctor, and because our society already focuses a good deal on medication, I'll spend less time on the biological side of things than the psychological and social ones. Yet, regardless of that approach, by the end of our journey together, I'll provide what I hope to be another mental health playbook — this one for taming and managing depression.

GET OUT OF YOUR HEAD . . . AGAIN?

In 2018, I published my first book, *Get Out of Your Head: A Toolkit for Living with and Overcoming Anxiety*. That work was a long-standing dream of mine, a goal I'd held since being diagnosed with anxiety in my teenage years. As I typed the final words of that manuscript, I expected to be ecstatic in the fulfillment of that dream. Yet, somehow, I found myself back inside my head, albeit, this time, in a different fashion.

To say I was surprised would be a total understatement. In my naive mind, I'd gotten to the bottom of this mental health thing, shared my insights with the world, and could now sit back and celebrate my achievement — or so I thought. In reality, I was staring into the eyes of my own dreaded sea monster.

In the fourteen months following that book's release, I rejoined the ranks of sufferers of the invisible illness of depression. I struggled mightily with melancholy — an old foe and one I never expected to see again. During those challenging months, I slowly began to change my outlook on being *done* with my writing efforts. My work was not complete — far from it. The mission I'd started just months prior, to help those struggling with their mental demons, was back on. And so, here we are again.

Since you're reading this, I imagine you've either struggled with depression previously or are experiencing it right now. Maybe you lost a friend or loved one, failed on a new business venture, or hit rock bottom for seemingly no reason at all. Whatever the cause, I've been there, too. To put it lightly, it's an extremely trying place to be.

Though some forms of the disease are undoubtedly worse than others, all depression is still, well, depression, and at the root of that insidious monster are the same awful feelings: pain, despair, and helplessness. Thus, regardless of how we become depressed, we can overcome it if we learn to outwit these daunting opponents.

These aren't just some feel-good words, either. Depression *is* beatable — please know that. No, maybe not a *shout from the rooftops* kind of beatable, but still, quietly and categorically surmountable. Though overcoming it takes time and dedication, it's conquerable nonetheless, and that's what I'll show you during our time together. But first, buckle up. We're heading into the storm.

WHAT IS THE ABYSS?

The reasons for our suffering are almost innumerable these days. In our new, digital age, we're constantly confronted by advertisements, push notifications, headlines, and social media posts. These messages continually remind us of our insufficiencies and try to convince us the world is going to hell in a handbasket.

Add these messages to the expected tribulations of life — career challenges, parenthood, uncertainty, disease, and death — and you get a society that, despite vast advances in medical and digital technologies, breeds despair at a rate previously unheard of in the civilized world.

And, if that's not enough, truly existential threats loom on the horizon. For example, researchers at Bain & Company, one of the world's top management consulting firms, estimate that by 2030, robots and other forms of artificial intelligence will displace up to 25% of jobs in America. These same folks also suggest that number could eventually grow to 50%.[11]

Worse yet, thanks to our overreliance on fossil fuels and the ongoing destruction of our ecosystems, we face the daunting possibility of global temperatures rising past the point of no return.[12] Thus, if we weren't dejected already, we now have the threat of a planet too hot to live on, with too few jobs to help us make ends meet. These truly are trying times.

While these concepts are undeniably terrifying, I don't state them to sink you into despair. I merely mention them to set the stage and prepare you for the battle ahead. These ideas once did, and at times still do, trigger my depression. They do for many of the people I talk to as well. However, as scary as they may be, we might as well get comfortable with them and figure out how to move past them. I said we were heading into the storm, after all, and I meant it.

In his influential work, *Beyond Good and Evil*, philosopher Friedrich Nietzsche stated, "If you gaze long into an abyss, the abyss also gazes into you."[13] Though there are many ways we can apply this statement to our lives, where I think it's particularly relevant is on the subject of depression. Unworthiness, grief, apocalyptic scenarios — each of these despair-filled subjects is an abyss in and of itself, an overwhelmingly deep, terrifying demander of our attention. And, like any abyss, the longer we stare into them, the more they look back into us, pulling us deeper and making us more miserable in the process.

In my last book, I used this exact quote to explain the subject of anxiety. In that work, I suggested it's not possible to "solve" fear. That is, the more we seek to analyze or outwit the things that scare us, the more confusing and frightening they become, both mentally and physically. The same, I'd argue, pertains to the things that spark our depression. Tighten our grip on those very things, and they will, in turn, tighten their grip on us. Stare into depressive thoughts and ideas, and those same concepts will tear apart not only our happiness but also, at times, our will to live.

Now, if you're wondering why this quote applies to both anxiety *and* depression, there are two compelling, main reasons. The first is that these diseases are closely related. Or, as industry experts say, they're the "fraternal twins of mood disorders."[14] Additionally, not only do both afflictions often appear together, but anxiety can also lead *to* depression. The second reason is that the human mind has its own abyss-like characteristics, from which these associated afflictions sometimes arise. Thus, this book is an exploration of how we fall into that abyss as well as a guide to navigating out of it.

To make the journey accompanying that exploration more amusing and relatable, I use the analogies of sailing the open seas and getting our boats pulled into actual maelstroms. Respectively, these concepts represent life in general and the sporadic appearance of depression in it. I'm sure these metaphors will feel a bit overdone at times, but, hey, I've always loved pirate ships and figure we might as well complete this arduous quest on a badass vessel with a swashbuckling mate or two.

For, it's those mates, both in the literal and metaphorical sense, who help us muster the courage to show up each day and work through our vortices, despite the lack of wind in our sails. Moreover, it's those same crew members who remind us, as the now trite meme often does, to "keep calm and carry on," not because it's necessarily the best strategy we have, but because, one day, if we stay the course, the abyss might throw us from its depths and launch us back into the harbor.

WHY THIS BOOK, AND WHY NOW?

It's not uncommon to hear that we live in the most incredible times in human history. After all, we can now fly from Los Angeles to New York in five hours, order products across the globe with the click of a button, and binge-watch the latest season of our favorite TV shows without even leaving the couch.

Yet while life has certainly become easier over the past few centuries, the real question is: has it gotten undeniably better? It depends on who you ask and how you look at things. On the other side of our technological advancements are some more daunting conclusions and bitter truths, such as the fact that instances of anxiety, depression, and suicide have skyrocketed in recent decades.[15] So much so, in fact, that in 2015, life expectancy in the US *decreased* for the first time since 1993.[16]

However, if there *is* an answer to this question, I think it's this: Yes, life is easier, freer, and more convenient than ever. It may even be better for most. But is it better for all? Sadly, I'd say *no*. Now, if that sounds negative, please stick with me for a bit. Though this book certainly has its gloomy parts, it's not pessimistic in the end. I promise we'll eventually come back to the light. We first just need to wade through the darkness.

Unfortunately, so many of us find ourselves drowning in that darkness regularly — myself included. That's why I wrote this book. Yes, amidst the hustle and bustle of prosperous, modern life, people all over the world are still suffering. These may be wonderful, opportune times we live in, but they're also difficult, unsettling, and tempestuous ones.

For evidence supporting that statement, we can look to our favorite celebrity news sources. Month after month, these outlets inform us of how yet another star — a person who, at least according to society, was the epitome of success and happiness — died via overdose or suicide. These stories are nothing short of tragic, and they speak to the crisis of despair currently sweeping through our nation.

They also show us, on both an individual and social level, things are broken. They make it clear that the system we've created, while unquestionably great in some respects, leaves many people out to dry. Sadly, that's one of the unfortunate byproducts of a society that doesn't adequately promote self-care.

Another one of those byproducts is that it's now quite challenging to talk about mental health. Few of us ever want to admit to *ourselves* we're struggling, never mind others. And yet, our inability to come clean about our conditions only seems to perpetuate them. We take our medication in private, run to and from our therapy sessions, and break into cold sweats at the thought of someone discovering our secrets. Yet, when we finally start talking, we realize many of us are suffering from the same dreaded afflictions. How relieved and connected that makes us feel.

I wrote this book to foster more of those conversations and make talking about depression a tad easier and less taboo. During these dark and divided times, we need much more of that. But, most importantly, I wrote it to give people hope. I wrote it to let you know there *is* life outside and beyond depression. Though the abyss may shield us from that truth at times, it's most certainly still there — and we're going to rediscover it together.

WHY SHOULD YOU LISTEN TO ME?

By traditional standards, I'm not exactly the leader of the pack when it comes to mental health. I didn't go to medical school. I'm not a social worker. I don't even have an undergraduate degree in psychology, never mind an advanced, clinical one. But thanks to the internet, the rules of the game have changed a bit as of late. No longer do you need a medical or graduate diploma to talk about depression. All you need is experience, a set of solutions, a computer, and an audience. Heck, even that last one might still be optional.

Luckily, I've got those things. If this is your first experience with my content, you probably want to know a little more about why I'm qualified to write a book like this one. Even if this isn't your first rodeo, you may still want a refresher. So, here goes.

Today, I'm a thirty-one-year-old software developer residing in Boston, Massachusetts. Yet, throughout my life, I've struggled with anxiety, depression, and a bit of obsessive-compulsive disorder. I always wondered why mental illness came for me. After all, I grew up in a moderately affluent suburb in Massachusetts, had an exceptional, opportunity-filled upbringing, and experienced little hardship outside of the typical challenges of everyday life.

As I got older, I asked myself, "Fortunate people couldn't get depressed, could they? And if they did, they should probably just keep their lucky mouths shut, right?" The answer, as I later discovered, was a resounding *no*.

From the day when I first considered those questions until now, I've interviewed people from all walks of life who struggle with mental illness themselves. As I've talked with those sufferers, consumed innumerable books and journal articles on the subject, and waded through my own difficulties, I've come to find that anxiety, depression, OCD, and the whole host of other mental illnesses do not discriminate. They can come for anyone, regardless of background, race, ethnicity, gender, or family history. Pretending they can't only makes them worse.

ANOTHER JOURNEY BEGINS

Since publishing the first entry in this *Get Out of Your Head* series — a treatise on overcoming anxiety — I've blogged regularly, across various websites, mainly about that same subject. And, as I mentioned in the opening pages of this book, I've started and finished another mental health battle, this time with depression. That battle is the main reason for this second installment in the series, and it's what we'll cover, in detail, in the next chapter.

Though our specific experiences with the disease, as well as life in general, have likely been quite different, we do, undoubtedly, have at least one thing in common: you and I both know suffering. No, I may not have been through all the same things you have. And, no, I'm not attempting to compare my past hurts with yours. All I'm trying to do is say that I, too, know what awful places the depths of the oceans are.

Thus, as you navigate these pages, as well as your own journey through depression, think of me not as a therapist but as a good friend. One who understands the struggle, has your best interests at heart, and, more than anything, just wants to see you happy again. I've done the research, charted the troubled waters, and worked diligently to present my findings to you. And, you, well, I think you've suffered long enough. Now, it's time to get through this thing together — and so we shall, as long as you're willing to let me guide you.

A PERFECT STORM

In the latter part of 2018, I experienced my first bout of depression in more than six years. Before I talk about that battle in detail, I want to provide two notes of caution on it. The first is that the story behind it — the one I'm about to tell — may be triggering for some, so, please, proceed at your own pace here. The last thing I'd want to do is reactivate or magnify your anguish. If anything in this story feels overwhelming, just skip to the next section or chapter.

The second is that I recite it merely to provide a backdrop for making sense of depression as a whole. I don't tell it to garner sympathy or suggest that what I've been through is worse than anything you've encountered. In reality, I know many of my readers have endured hardships I couldn't even fathom. Thus, despite our potential differences in background, upbringing, and experience, remember, I'm recounting this tale solely in an attempt to help you. And so, with those thoughts, and a bit of caution, let's begin.

It was September of 2018, and I had a couple of old roommates in town. One of my friends, Jim, invited us all on his boat for the afternoon. It was shaping up to be the last opportunity of the season; we couldn't miss it. We hit the liquor store, grabbed a few cases of beer, and emptied them into the boat's coolers prior to undocking.

A PERFECT STORM

After pulling out of Boston's Seaport, we cruised around for an hour, then decided we wanted to jump in the ocean. To make our swims a bit warmer and more appealing, we dropped anchor near one of the city's small beaches. It was a beautiful day, with not a cloud in the sky. We blasted upbeat music from the boat's speakers in celebration.

Once we'd had our fill of the water, we reboarded our vessel and invited various onlooking women to venture toward us for a drink. It was honestly kind of hilarious. Most weekends, we'd go to the bar and barely stand out. But, on this particular weekend, thanks to the boat, we could somehow entice any swim-happy woman on the beach. We all laughed and clinked glasses as we realized yet another group of young ladies was heading our way.

It was one of those capstone kinds of days, one for which we'd all, in some fashion, worked quite hard. My friend Jim, who owned the boat, had toiled for years on a technology startup before selling a few shares to an investor. With some of his profits, he treated himself to the vessel that enabled our fantastic trip that day.

Another friend onboard, Sean, was in a similar situation. Though he was once a relatively anxious entrepreneur, he persisted through years of stress to bring his biotech company to the forefront of Boston's startup scene. And while he wasn't immediately heading toward fame and fortune, he was well-positioned with a handsome salary, an ownership stake in his company, and a smart, driven girlfriend.

And then there was me. Though I, too, was a recovering nervous wreck, I'd been relatively happy since a battle with depression six years prior. In the years following that battle, I worked through my biggest insecurities and eventually landed a long-desired role as a software consultant. And, to top it all off, I'd just put the finishing touches on the final draft of what I believed to be the most important work of my life: my first book and the initial entry in the series you're now reading.

About ninety minutes into our beach trip — just after our new friends had returned ashore — Jim, Sean, and I looked at one another in disbelief. Despite not saying a thing, we all knew it: how fortunate we were to be making friends, basking in the sun, and drinking beer on the back of a boat. And all on a Sunday, nonetheless.

Sean was the first to break our awe-filled silence. "How unbelievable is this?! What did we do to get so lucky? And to think, we're all heading to Europe together in just over a week! I'm not sure life can get any better. I feel like something has to go horribly wrong, very soon, because this doesn't make any sense." Though I didn't concur with his last statement, I did agree we were fortunate. Perhaps exceptionally so.

Jim was next. He turned back toward us as he simultaneously pulled up the anchor. "Sean's right. Today's been amazing, and we are incredibly lucky. But it's getting late, so we should probably head home." Then, he walked over to the driver's seat, revved the engine, and started doing doughnuts. I watched as a mini whirlpool formed around us. "Okay, guys, one last jump if anyone wants it!"

Desperate to savor as much of that day as I could, I sprang up and ran toward the back of the vessel. As I went to make my final plunge into the ocean, I stopped and pondered what Sean had said just moments prior. I thought to myself, "We seriously are lucky. Barring a tragedy or horrific loss in my life, I can't see how this happiness train could possibly stop rolling." And, with that thought, I dove off the stern, into the small gyre surrounding us.

THE CHASM OPENS

Every Autumn, in the town where my parents live, a semi-famous fair pops up for a couple of weeks. I've attended it for as long as I can remember. In elementary and middle school, my folks would take my brother and me annually. We'd play the traditional carnival games, jump on a few rides, pet some farm animals, and consume the standard, terrible-for-you-but-awesome assortments of candy, fried foods, and soda.

In high school, we'd also go, but this time, at night — either by driving ourselves or hitching a ride with one of our schoolmates. The fair at night was just like it was during the day, filled with games, rides, and junk food. However, after sunset, there was a new twist: the boy-girl dynamic.

Being stuck in class all week made it difficult to socialize with or pursue some of the females in which we'd taken a romantic interest. Luckily, the fair presented us with a well-timed and much-needed opportunity. No parents. No teachers. Just a bunch of foolish high school boys trying to impress the girls on whom they had crushes.

When I look back on all those good times, I can't help but feel a bit nostalgic. The early visits with Mom and Dad, tomfoolery with classmates, prize-winning basketball shots, alluring carnival lights, and first kisses. Those memories will stick with me forever.

That's why, a few days after the boat trip with my friends, when my brother texted me and asked if I wanted to go to the fair with his family, I jumped at the idea. The following Sunday, we drove up to it, then spent the afternoon showing his son around, eating apple cider doughnuts, and petting all the animals.

As we were getting ready to leave, my nephew pointed at the carousel, signaling that he wanted to go on it. I volunteered to take him. We waited until it was our turn, then climbed up onto the ride and laughed as it kicked into gear. It was one of those magic moments where time kind of disappears. I stood there, relishing my nephew's glee, thinking to myself, "Wow. I remember when my parents took me on this same carousel. It feels like it was just yesterday. Where did the time go?"

When the merry-go-round finally came to a complete stop, I helped my nephew down from the horse on which he was sitting and walked him back over to the rest of the group. From there, we slowly headed to the parking lot, said goodbye to one another, and drove our separate ways back to our respective homes.

That night, as I sat on the couch in my Boston apartment, I saw my phone light up with a notification. It was an email. The subject line read, "Hey, Brian, does this look familiar?" Intrigued, I opened it as fast as I could. In the body of that message was the password to my Gmail account. The message's sender said he'd hacked into my computer and retrieved it, along with all my other login credentials and sensitive information. I was spooked.

But that wasn't even the worst of it; my new pen pal also said he'd taken hours of video from my computer's webcam and pulled all the contacts off my hard drive. And, if I didn't send him $2,000 worth of cryptocurrency within twenty-four hours, he'd forward footage of me visiting adult websites to everyone in my address book.

Now, I know it may sound hilarious or like an obvious scam to you today, but trust me, this email was tactfully worded. Moreover, its sender had already convinced me he'd done what he'd claimed. After all, he had my Gmail password. How else could he have gotten it other than by hacking into my computer?

For five minutes straight, I did precisely what you'd think I did. I completely and thoroughly freaked out. You know, the kind where you sweat so hard that, if someone walked into the room, he or she would think you'd just gotten back from marathon training? Yeah, that kind.

Despite the anxiety, I resolved not to do anything drastic until I'd calmed down. The hacker said he wouldn't send the video for twenty-four hours anyway, so I had some time to think this one over. If I could get myself in a less frantic state, I figured, then maybe I could look at this situation in a new light. I practiced some deep breathing for a few minutes, then concluded I should see if anyone on the internet had reported something similar in the past. Luckily, they had.

When I typed the concept into Google, I found that this specific email was part of a relatively new and widespread set of phishing attacks on the internet. Essentially, hackers would pay for aggregated databases of compromised email addresses and passwords, then bulk-send the message I'd received to all those addresses.

Since I'd carelessly used the same credentials across the web, I'd all but guaranteed that if this person discovered any *one* of my passwords, it'd be the same as the one to my email account and, in turn, corroborate the rest of his story. In other words, the password he'd obtained likely came from one of the many smaller, less secure sites I'd signed up for previously — not Gmail.

Upon making that realization, I breathed a huge sigh of relief, closed my phone, vowed to change my passwords the next day, and headed upstairs for bed. Before turning off the lights, however, I navigated to one of my favorite technology news websites: *TechCrunch*.

Smack dab on its front page was a popular meme — the one with the cartoon dog saying to himself, "this is fine," while sitting in a flame-engulfed kitchen. I always laugh when I see it, so I clicked on the post to which it pertained. I had no idea what I was about to get myself into. Almost immediately, the article got very dark. While still in a bit of fight-or-flight from the phishing fiasco just minutes prior, I zoomed through the story in a frenzy of fear.

As I read, I realized the article was, for the most part, a summation of the recently published *National Climate Assessment*, foretelling ecological gloom, doom, and devastation.[17] It warned that humanity's carbon footprint was destroying the earth, and very quickly at that. In addition, it argued that if we didn't radically change how we lived and consumed energy, the planet would heat up rapidly and irreversibly in the coming century — all but sealing our collective fate.

Though I'd already been on high alert after the email scare, I was now completely freaked out and overwhelmed. The thoughts, doubts, and questions fired non-stop. I started sweating profusely again and felt like I couldn't breathe. I was damn near having a panic attack, something I hadn't experienced in close to ten years. I just couldn't shake what I'd read and the existential dread it'd sparked in me.

While I'd previously experienced such dread on smaller scales, I'd always gotten through it by reassuring myself that everything in this world eventually coming to an end was simply a part of the circle of life. And, as I'd written in the manuscript I'd completed just days earlier, that concept of transitoriness can sometimes be a good thing. For example, even our most anxiety-provoking moments, though quite challenging to get through, eventually pass and bring us relief. Moreover, when we later look back on our lives, we often find that these events didn't turn out to be such big deals in the long run.

However, the core concept from that *TechCrunch* article didn't fit this mold or yield to my quiet reassurances. After all, this wasn't some in-the-moment or passing concern it was addressing. This was the entire circle of life. The very notion that we could pollute the planet into annihilation — it was an idea so morbid and depressing my brain couldn't process it. I fixated on it for hours that night, only to find that, with each pass through, I fell deeper and deeper into misery. I didn't realize it at the time, but this was precisely what Nietzsche had warned of: the godforsaken abyss.

CIRCLING AROUND THE VORTEX

My mood didn't change much the following morning; in fact, the next few days were some of the most difficult I've ever experienced. What only added to my sense of despair was that I knew my life was still, by traditional standards, splendid. Unlike many folks who battle the leviathan of depression, I hadn't lost a family member or job or even faced some unspeakable tragedy. I'd just fallen into such a terrible state that I'd begun to look at life, in general, as one.

In addition, I'd recently landed the flexible, well-paying job I'd sought for so long. As such, I could work almost anytime I wanted, from anywhere. Most days, that place ended up being my three-bedroom apartment, which I virtually had to myself since my roommates were never around. Yet, despite those freedoms, somehow, I still wasn't content. I'd tell friends about my work and living situations, and they'd all say, "Are you kidding me? That sounds amazing. I'm so jealous." Talk about cognitive dissonance.

Worse yet, I'd just completed the manuscript for my first book, one in which I'd told folks how to overcome anxiety. Yet, here I was, completely miserable myself. I felt like a total fraud, and the worst part was, I never even saw it coming. I asked myself, "How am I supposed to publish a book about mental health when I'm not mentally healthy right now? Am I just an ungrateful heap of garbage, or is this happiness thing not all it's cracked up to be?" Though they were undoubtedly dark questions, I couldn't push them out of my mind at the time.

I was in a complete spiral. I didn't even want to go to Europe with my friends anymore. I packed my bags halfheartedly, leaving several necessary items at home by accident. I also forgot to call my parents before takeoff. I should've been ecstatic for that vacation, but I was in such a bad place, mentally, that even the excursion of a lifetime felt like just another part of the nightmare.

Right before I left for the airport, I looked across my room at a picture of my nephew and me. The same nephew I'd taken on the carousel just days earlier. At that moment, all my memories at the fair over the years came rushing back. The emotions, too. "Could those trips seriously have been five, eleven, even fifteen years ago? Where the heck did the time go? And when did I get so old?" It seemed, at least for the moment, like life was passing by right before my eyes. I wondered, would the next few decades go just as fast?

I prayed my vacation would be the very thing I needed to reset and return to baseline. I knew I'd be in the comfort of friends, checking various items off my bucket list. Unfortunately, on that trip, I learned that when you're in a dark place, not even the most enticing experiences will shelter you from the noise in your mind. Physically, I was there with my friends the whole time, but mentally, I was on another planet.

It was the saddest and least hopeful I'd ever been in my life, almost every hour of the day, for days on end. Though there were certainly moments of relief, for the most part, I spent that entire trip in my head. Spurred by my run-in with the climate report just days earlier, I fixated on life, death, and the significance of it all. I thought to myself, "If we all die one day, and if we could damage the environment so much that we wipe humanity off the face of the earth, then is there any inherent meaning to this thing we call existence?"

It was a terrible question and one I shouldn't have asked myself. But I did anyway. That meant I had to deal with the consequences. As I spiraled further and further into bleakness, I thought about what the opposite of death would mean — to live forever. That idea scared me almost as much as death itself, and so, I found myself in a complete mental pretzel, not wanting to die but not totally wanting to live, either.

It's a good thing I had my friends around. Their constant companionship and energy on that vacation were the only things that kept me going through the madness. Though I remained in the depths of my mind for most of that trip, I pushed through to the end, telling myself that, when I returned home, I'd feel safer and less overwhelmed. And, in many ways, I did. At least until I got a call from my mother a few days later.

She told me my grandmother, who'd been on and off hospice for years, had finally taken a turn for the worse. Now, she appeared to be just days from passing. I always knew the time would come when I'd have to say goodbye to her, and it hung over me for a good portion of my life.

There are few individuals with whom I've ever been closer than my grandmother. She was one of the nicest, most loving, and most supportive people I've ever met. She was also one of the strongest. She battled through several cancer diagnoses and thirteen years of chemotherapy and dementia-related pain to be there for her family. Throughout those thirteen years, I dreaded the thought of going on without her, of living without her strength, love, and joy.

The night before I left for Europe, I visited her at her nursing home, just in case she passed while I was gone. On that visit, I saw a person who'd been through so much and was so tired. I almost broke down right in the middle of that visit. It just didn't seem fair — a saint of a woman losing her cognitive capacities and will to live. The sight alone crushed my spirits and sunk me deeper into my depression.

In my youth, my grandmother was always there, at my sports games and graduations, cheering me on. And, even later in life, after she lost the ability to leave the house, she was always waiting for my phone calls, eager to send her love and listen to me talk about my problems.

When that dreaded day finally came, I was already so numb I didn't know how to handle another disappointment in life. It felt like I was in the middle of an inescapable, perfect storm, sinking into its whirlpool while praying for the clouds to part. It wasn't until I returned to my empty apartment after her services that it hit me. Nana was gone. One of my closest friends and biggest supporters in life wasn't there anymore. I felt so alone, so hopeless and dejected.

I wish I could say I resolved to overcome my depression and gracefully righted the ship immediately following those services. That wouldn't be truthful, however. In reality, the depression I faced before *and* after my grandmother's passing was a battle that raged on for more than a year. And, if I'm being frank, it's one that still surfaces briefly, in slightly different ways, every now and then.

I'd also be lying if I said I came up with the magic formula for instantly conquering all types of depression during that same battle. As I mentioned in the previous chapter, such a formula does not yet exist. There's a reason for this, and it's that depression is a complex, multifaceted disorder. In many cases, we find it's not one thing in particular that drives someone into despair. Instead, it's a combination of changes, losses, or shortcomings in one's biological, psychological, and social worlds.

A PERFECT STORM

That's also why overcoming depression can be a long haul — rebuilding all three of those worlds takes time.

Now, if that sounds daunting, let me assure you, not all is lost here. There's plenty of good news as well. While I don't have the *magic* formula for defeating depression, I do have a set of strategies we can leverage. Those strategies are what I discovered and developed during the year-long journey I just recounted. They're also what we'll cover throughout the rest of this book.

As we'll see during the unfolding of them, once we've persevered through an extended bout of depression, we realize that getting through subsequent ones is indeed possible. That gives us hope. Sometimes, we even come out of our spells with insights on how to approach the next ones. And, thankfully, since the biopsychosocial model works in a synergistic fashion, when we start to rebuild any one of our biological, psychological, or social worlds, we also confer benefits onto the remaining two.

That wide array of benefits is one of the main things we'll focus on during our time together. But first, we have to lay some necessary groundwork — we must define what depression is and how it emerges in our lives. And so, with that in mind, let's continue this maritime adventure and sail on into the vast expanses of the mental health ocean.

THE STATE OF THE WATER

If you've suffered from depression in the past or are encountering some form of it right now, you don't exactly need me to tell you what it is. After all, having experienced it means you've come to understand what a dark and terrifying force it can be. Yet, even though many of us are familiar with this foe, I still think we should define and break it down further.

There are a few reasons for this, the first one being that I want folks who are brand new to this battle to be able to make sense of what they're currently facing. The second is that, by explaining what depression is, we'll create a common language we can use to talk about it in greater detail. And the final one is that, in having such a discussion, we'll uncover a handful of insights we can apply to our own struggles or those of someone we love.

Of course, I *could* begin that discussion by diving into the granddaddy of all psychiatric publications — the *Diagnostic and Statistical Manual of Mental Disorders (the DSM)* — the "Rosetta Stone," if you will, for categorizing and identifying mental illnesses. I *could* also explore how that manual provides a list of despair-related symptoms and requires that patients exhibit five or more of them for two weeks before a doctor can diagnose Clinical Depression — a condition also referred to as Major Depressive Disorder (MDD).[18]

However, I'm *not* going to do that for two reasons. The first is that MDD isn't the only variation of depression. The second is that I don't want to make this subject more complicated than it already is or needs to be. Many researchers feel this way about the affliction as well.[19] And while I think having a framework for classifying any disease is critical for doctors and patients alike, I disagree that depression must always fit into a specific, particular box.

For example, if we only exhibit four of the following related symptoms — depressed mood, loss of interest in most activities, fluctuations in weight or appetite, interruptions in sleep patterns, slowing of physical movements, persistent fatigue, feelings of worthlessness, decreased concentration, or recurring thoughts of death — can we really say we aren't depressed?[20] Again, I'm no medical professional, but the fact that non-MDD varieties of the disease exist seems to suggest the answer to that question is *no*.

In the end, we're the ones who know how we feel. That means, when we're down in the dumps for an extended period, it's up to us to seek the proper help, regardless of what some list might tell us. Of course, no reasonable physician would think or operate in such a rigid fashion, either; the main job of all our doctors is to serve and support us, and that'll always come ahead of the DSM's criteria.

Yet, that doesn't mean there isn't still a potential problem in getting treated, and that problem comes down to how *we* view our conditions. When we look at the DSM's guidelines and use them to decide whether or not we should visit our physicians in the first place, we run the risk of falling short of its standards and preventing ourselves from getting the help we need. Such should never be the case, no matter what *any* manual has to say.

But I digress. After all, my goal here is not to get lost in the minutiae — it's just to talk about the common threads of depression's various forms. In doing so, I'll seek to help you make more sense of the affliction overall and develop powerful strategies for managing it. That sentiment applies regardless of whether you're dealing with Major Depressive Disorder, Postpartum Depression, Bipolar Disorder, or something similar.

With that slight detour behind us, let's finally give a clear definition of what depression is. At its core, the word "depression" refers to either a dark emotional state or one of several clinical mood disorders in which we feel both helpless and hopeless at the same time. Though there are innumerable symptoms associated with each type of the disease, just about all of them boil down to these two terrible emotions, which is why they'll be a focal point of our discussion as we move forward.

Over the past century, countless experiments and research projects have reaffirmed this simplified definition of the complex condition. However, few of them are more well-known than those of Dr. Martin Seligman, the father of positive psychology. Through his most famous study, Seligman sought to understand how animals respond to stress in different environments.[21]

In the first part of that study, he placed two sets of dogs in separate, lever-equipped boxes and subjected them to painful,

31

electric shocks. There was a marked difference in each group's box, however, and it was that, for the first set, pressing the lever ended the painful stimuli, whereas, for the second, doing so didn't change a thing. Thus, to the latter group, it appeared as though the shocks simply ended at random.

In the second segment of the experiment, Seligman removed the levers and added a short dividing wall to his boxes. On one side of them, the side where he placed his dogs, shocks surged just as they did in the first part of the trial. On the other side, however, there were no such stressors. Thus, Seligman wanted to see if his canines would jump over the wall in an attempt to evade their pain. The results, if you haven't heard them already, were quite interesting.

In essence, the dogs who had the power to manually stop their shocks in the first half of the experiment quickly discovered the ability to hurdle the wall and escape them in the second. However, those who couldn't stop them initially didn't come to such a realization. Instead, they merely sat down, whimpered, and endured the distress.

This behavior the whimpering dogs exhibited is what came to be known as *learned helplessness*.[22] It's the idea that we, or any other animal, for that matter, can become disempowered and discouraged when our environments don't respond to our efforts in the fashions we desire. So discouraged, in fact, we decide taking action is no longer a viable option.

In the years following Seligman's experiment, more and more researchers drew connections between learned helplessness and depression. Their conclusion? When difficult-to-control stressors arise in our lives, we tend to grow doubtful of our ability to change them and sink into states of despair and melancholy.[23] That's why I and so many others say depression is mainly an affliction of helplessness and hopelessness; while there's certainly more to it as well, if we strip any form of the disease down to its core, we'll almost always find these two hallmark-like feelings.

Interestingly enough, the duration and degree to which we're experiencing these emotions also help determine which variety of the condition we're facing.[24] For example, Seasonal Affective Disorder (SAD) tends to be an acute form of depression that lasts for a few specific months.[25] In contrast, Persistent Depressive Disorder (dysthymia) is usually less severe but extends for two or more years at a time.[26] The same logic applies to categorizing many other varieties as well, including MDD and bipolar disorder.

If you've previously wrestled with depression in your own life, I'd imagine you can relate to these basic concepts. For example, if you've ever fallen into despair after losing a loved one, you'll know the disease tries to tell you you'll never be happy again without the person you lost, and that, no matter what you do, you'll always remain in your current state. That said, assuming you've navigated such an onerous situation before, you'll also know these feelings and beliefs tend to fade away over time, regardless of what your mental demons suggest.

The problem, however, is that when we're in the middle of a depressive episode, it's hard for us to see that things actually will get better. Instead, we assume our unwanted present conditions and feelings will subsist forever. We make this assumption not because we're uncreative or foolish but because the pain of our depression overwhelms us and inhibits our ability to think and see clearly. This blurriness is not only one of the most challenging things about dealing with the affliction — it's also a key characteristic of the abyss itself.

THE RETURN OF THE STATE MACHINE

If you read the first book in this series, you'll know I'm a bit of a computer science nerd. In that book, I introduced a vital programming concept called *the state machine*.[27] Before we remind ourselves of the details behind such a concept, we must revisit the principle upon which it operates. That principle is the idea that the ways by which computers and their applications work are contingent upon their current states.

Now, I'm guessing that makes *some* sense to you but also feels pretty abstract. Don't worry. We'll turn this idea into something more concrete with the following real-world example. Let's say you're playing a computer game that mimics a slot machine. This game takes a digital coin as its fee to play and, as such, has two states: *coin inserted* and *coin not inserted*. Since the game runs as, or on top of, a state machine, it'll take different actions depending upon whether it's collected such a fee.

Specifically, when it boots up and detects that you haven't yet inserted a token, it'll make sounds and show animations alerting you to such a fact. It'll also continue to do so until you actually insert one. Moreover, if you try to spin the slot machine before relinquishing a coin, it'll present a dialogue stating that you're *still* not ready to begin.

Once you cough up your payment, however, the machine will transition to its *coin inserted* state and alter its appearance. Its badgering sounds and animations will transform into tunes and messages of excitement, prompting you to give the reels a spin. When you attempt to begin your turn in this state, the game will grant your request and put those reels in motion. Then, after they stop moving, the system will reward you with any potential winnings you've earned, recalculate which state it should be in, and start the process all over again.

Though a real slot machine game is a bit more complicated than what I just described, I find it helpful to start small when trying to make sense of technical ideas like the one we're discussing here — hence the simplified example. So, taking what we covered, we can now go back and redeclare what a state machine is. Specifically, it's an object's state-based instruction manual. It describes all of that object's potential configurations and explains how that thing performs in and navigates to and from each one.

Okay, so we've got that part figured out, but just what does all this computer science talk have to do with depression? I'm glad you asked. Since depression is a mood disorder, we can say that when we're experiencing it, we're in a depressed mood or state. And when we're in that state — or any state for that matter —

there should exist some behavior or set of actions we can take to move out of it, into a new one. These actions are our figurative insertings of coins into our slot machines.

As with all states, depression-related ones can and do change. This is evident in the fact that, even though we live mainly in realms of despair and hopelessness when we're melancholic, there are still fleeting moments where we leave such places temporarily. Thus, on a general level, we can say that the more often we're able to pull ourselves out of those terrible mindsets, the better chance we have of escaping our depression altogether.

Of course, despair and hopelessness can be incredibly intense and resistant feelings. Therefore, even though I claim it's possible to evade our depression by changing our state, I'm not saying such a task is easy or simply no big deal. Though I understand it could come off that way, trust me, the last thing I'd ever intend to do is downplay or trivialize what you or anyone else is going through.

At the same time, however, that potential miscommunication doesn't change the fact that even when we're depressed, there is *something* we can do to outrun our predicaments. Sure, it might not always be apparent what that thing is, and it might take a lot of time and effort to carry out once we discover it, but still, that *something* exists in either the biological, psychological, or social spheres of our lives.

That's why, as we move forward, we'll continue to discuss state-changing strategies from all three of our model's spheres. In

36

doing so, we'll identify the ones that resonate with us the most and begin to rewrite our internal instruction manuals for traversing difficult emotions. That way, any time we land in an unhelpful or destructive state in the future, we'll have reliable tactics at our disposal that we can utilize to navigate ourselves to more positive places.

Though this idea of methodically leveraging specific actions to change our states is undoubtedly important for us and our mental health, it's not the only one that helps us connect state machines to depression in general. There's a second one at play here as well, and it should come as no surprise, as it's both very closely related to the principle upon which state machines operate and something we've quietly covered already.

That idea is that, just like computers and their applications, our current state governs how we behave in almost any situation. For us, this means that, when we're in a depressed state, we're likely thinking, feeling, and acting in different fashions than we would if we were in a more uplifting one. While it may sound simple, I'd argue that, beneath the surface, this second notion is even more impactful in terms of how we view and manage depression than the first. For, as we'll see in a moment, our current frame of mind also influences how we make sense of what's happening around us, and, with the wrong determinations, we can keep ourselves down in the abyss for far too long.

THE POWER OF OUR CURRENT STATE

Out of this second connection-fostering lesson emerges one of the more crucial concepts we'll discuss in this book — the fact that we perceive the world not as it is but as we are. That is, we interpret the events unfolding around us subjectively rather than objectively, based on how we're feeling, what we believe, what we learned as children, and so on. Or, to draw from an old, popular saying: when we think we're a hammer, everything looks like a nail — even if it's not.[28]

If this concept isn't evident just yet or its application to depression still seems a bit tenuous, that's okay. We'll cover a few real-life examples in the pages ahead that'll help put this theoretical idea into practice and make it more relatable. The first of those examples, somewhat unexpectedly, comes from the golf course.

Now, I'm a pretty terrible golfer, but if there's one thing I excel at while on the links, it's in thinking I've lost one of my clubs. This isn't all that uncommon in the sport, however, as the end of almost any hole provides players an easy opportunity to leave an iron behind. Here's what I mean by that.

Since carts aren't allowed near the green, golfers tend to park their vehicles well before it and carry a wedge and putter with them toward the cup, saving themselves a trip back to their bags between short shorts. While this strategy speeds up the pace of play, it also lends itself to the problem I just mentioned. That is, sometimes, players chip onto the green, drop their wedges, putt to completion, and hurry back to their carts, not realizing they've abandoned their poor irons.

That's why, whenever I finish a hole, I try to remember to do a quick club check to make sure I didn't succumb to this mistake myself. Yet since I rarely keep the fourteen or so sticks in my bag organized, I often find myself peering down at my set, thinking, "Oh no, I'm missing my wedge." With that declaration, I put myself in a panic-stricken state.

Once in that frame of mind, I look frantically around my golf bag, hoping to see the club I think I've left behind. Simultaneously, I retrace my steps in my head, trying to determine the hole on which I could've possibly lost it. Funny enough, however, it's usually sitting right there in my bag in front of me. The only problem is, I can't see it because I'm too preoccupied with worrying about where I lost it in the first place.

This sort of thing is what I mean when I say we perceive the world not as it is but as we are. When we're full of fear, we can't see the forest for the trees or the ocean for the waves. Or, in this example, we simply can't see our club. More often than not, if we stay in our frantic, fearful state, it'll take us some time to realize we haven't actually lost our iron. When we instead step back, breathe, and clear our heads, we change our perceptions, and that club makes itself apparent to us once again.

Surprisingly, there's a term for this sort of lapse in sight, and it's called a *scotoma*. In the literal sense, this word describes an area of our vision that's become partially or fully diminished via disease or degeneration. When used metaphorically, however, the expression refers to a more psychological blind spot or discrepancy between perception and reality. As we've seen, one of the potential reasons for that discrepancy is the state in which we find ourselves.

Now, of course, not all of us are golfers, so this first example might not necessarily resonate with everyone. Thankfully, however, these kinds of lessons are a fairly common takeaway from research studies, meaning there's plenty of similar stories to go around. Take, for instance, the following example on grocery shopping behavior.

In a 1969 study, researchers found that individuals of normal weight who hadn't recently eaten tended to buy more food at the supermarket than those who had.[29] As the logic goes, when participants were hungry, their cravings pushed them to stray from their grocery lists and buy whatever sounded good at the moment. In other words: almost everything in the store.

While this takeaway helps many of us humorously relate to one of our most commonly shared blunders, it also does something else — it epitomizes the influence our feelings exert over our behaviors. We see this phenomenon play out not just while food shopping but also in many other areas of our lives. For example, when we're stuffed or hungover, we tell ourselves we'll never eat or imbibe again. And yet, eventually, we recover from our temporary ailments, move into new states, and enjoy yet another meal or beverage, despite what we'd told ourselves.

There's a reason we repeatedly fall prey to these oversights, and it's that we often subconsciously assume that the state we're in will never change. Whatever that state may be — depression included — it narrows our line of sight, blinding us to a myriad of possibilities.

To put it another way, we often make evaluations and decisions based on how we feel while forgetting that those feelings are fluid. As such, we sometimes promise we'll never repeat a specific behavior simply because we can't see past our current emotions and circumstances. Though this may not sound like a scotoma, it is. It's our state temporarily impairing our view of the world. Eventually, our emotions will change — and so will that outlook — whether we realize it or not.

While I enjoy these fun and basic scotoma illustrations, I'm certainly aware that they don't directly apply to the subject of depression. To make that connection in full and prove that this concept isn't just some random, unrelated idea, I'll need a couple more examples. Luckily, I've got some, the first of which comes from a study conducted in 1983.[30]

In that study, a group of researchers performed two experiments. These two trials sought to determine whether participants' moods influenced their perception of reality. In the first one, scientists asked subjects to recall either sad or happy memories from their past, then state how satisfied they were with their lives, in general.

In the second one, administrators first told participants to describe the weather outside, then followed up with the same life-satisfaction-style questions as before. In this second trial, scientists highlighted the sunniness or raininess of the day, hoping to bait participants into good and bad moods, respectively.

To tie the experiments together, the administrators placed several participants from trial one into trial two. Then, during the latter, they lured such subjects into the opposite mood from that of the former. For example, if they prompted someone to divulge a sad memory in trial one, they'd then phone that same person on a beautiful day and call attention to its sunniness in trial two.

Doing such a thing allowed the study's conductors to connect life satisfaction responses across both experiments and see if participants changed their answers based on the mood into which each one persuaded them. After all, those who'd recently claimed to be unsatisfied with their lives couldn't possibly report something different just a short time later, could they?

Upon finishing their investigations, the experimenters concluded that was very much the case. Specifically, they found that participants would, more often than not, flip-flop on their life satisfaction responses from the first trial to the second when induced into opposite moods in each one. In other words, what researchers asked participants to discuss tended to alter their overall outlooks on life, regardless of what they'd previously reported.

And while we can't know for sure that these same folks didn't have more legitimate reasons for changing their answers, this study seems to support a core premise of our discussions in this chapter. That premise is that the mood or state we're in influences, even determines, how we evaluate our lives, at both a high and low level. More importantly, when those evaluations are negative, we set the stage for the harmful, follow-on kind of thinking that causes the abyss to emerge.

Thus, if there's one key takeaway from all of these discussions, it seems to be this: It's of the utmost importance that we regularly monitor how we're feeling and change our state, as necessary, to avoid or escape such mental whirlpools. Though we'll continue to uncover ways to do just that in the chapters ahead, for now, let's remember that even *simple* shifts in our internal and external environments can sometimes improve our mood and pull us from our ruminative depths.

Now, of course, not all depression comes and goes from such simple shifts, nor am I claiming that it does. All I'm saying is that when we're depressed, we're in disempowering, wretched frames of mind. And while getting out of those frames is often quite challenging, that arduousness doesn't mean they're unchangeable or that we'll be stuck in them forever. It may certainly feel that way in the moment, but that's usually just our current state blinding us and painting the world black — not reality. Once the sun comes back out, we'll be able to take our blinders off and view things optimistically yet again.

These state-related conclusions I'm making aren't a one-off sort of thing, either. There are plenty of other experiments that have reaffirmed this kind of thinking before. For example, take this 1988 study that attempted to determine how easily various groups of people can recall positive and negative upcoming occurrences.[31] In that study, researchers split participants into three groups — those experiencing anxiety, those experiencing a mix of anxiety and depression, and a control group not experiencing either — then asked each one to brainstorm some forthcoming events and recorded the results.

What they found was, when compared to the control group, the anxious cohort could more easily recall undesirable upcoming situations. In addition, the mixed anxious-depressed group not only thought up more of the same kind of events but also struggled to brainstorm as many positive ones.

While the researchers drew several conclusions from this experiment, one of them was right in line with what we've been hammering home throughout this chapter — the state we're in, whether anxious, depressed, or something else, influences how we perceive our world and the events within it. When we're melancholic, even the typically fun happenings on our calendars, such as going to baseball games with friends, don't look very appealing.

Though it can be difficult to stomach this inability to get excited about such normally enjoyable things, two specific facts help us navigate that difficulty with greater composure. The first is that this temporary lack of excitement is a hallmark of depression and not some other abnormality. The second is that this same dearth of enthusiasm is merely a product of our depressed state, not our temperament. Once we feel better, we'll see those games in a more hopeful light.

When we remind ourselves of these facts while in despair, we slow our psychological currents and invite that light to break through our mental clouds a bit more rapidly. However, when we do the opposite, we make ourselves vulnerable to both the abyss and another cyclical process that proves harder to get out of as we move through it. That process is what we'll spend the next chapter discussing.

INTO THE CURRENT

In the last chapter, we asserted that our current state paints our world and influences our perception of it. As it relates to depression, this is a critical determination to make since it tells us that how we feel right now doesn't always equal reality. Moreover, it suggests that if we can change our frame of mind, we may also change how reality presently appears.

If we extrapolate this relationship between state management and perception out one level further, we come to an even more important concept — something I call the Perception Cycle. The funny thing about this concept is we've basically covered it already. We just haven't referred to it by name.

To explain what I mean by that, let's quickly revisit our golf story from the previous chapter. In that story, I described a fear-inspired blunder I occasionally make on the course. It goes something like this: Knowing that golfers often leave irons on the green, I regularly inspect my bag to ensure I didn't fall prey to such a mistake myself. Yet since I rarely organize my clubs properly, I sometimes look down at them and declare I've lost one when, in fact, I just haven't spotted it yet.

That declaration then puts me in a worry-filled state, which further inhibits me from locating my club and forces me to question where I could've possibly left it in the first place. Such questioning then reinforces my franticness and causes me to fret about that club yet again. And so the pattern repeats, at least until I take a breath and calmly count up my irons or do something else to break myself out of such a loop.

This rough sequence of feeling, thinking, acting, and evaluating is the essence of the Perception Cycle — a behavioral-model-like concept that suggests the following: Our current state determines what we tell ourselves, which influences the actions we do or don't take in our lives. Such actions then impact the results we get, which, finally, affect our state and start the process all over again. Or, in other words, how we see the world and what's happening around us remains virtually the same until we change our frame of mind, develop a new game plan, or achieve an outcome that alters either of those things.

As it pertains to depression, the cycle unfolds a bit like this: First, we fall into or find ourselves in a bleak, hopeless state. As such, our outlooks on the world and the stories we tell ourselves about our conditions follow that bleakness.

These desolate inner dialogues then inform our next course of action. When we're depressed, such a course typically takes the shape of further obsessing over destructive ideas and possibilities, mindlessly consuming digital media, halfheartedly attempting to engage in something productive, or simply doing nothing at all.

After carrying out whichever of these unimaginative game plans we so choose, we realize our conditions haven't changed all that much; we're still in the same hopeless state. From that state, we restart the process once more, only this time, with even less hope than we had previously. After all, we told ourselves it'd be nearly impossible to get out of our funk, and we proved it. So, what would make us think the result would be any different next time around?

Though that question is rhetorical, it illustrates an interesting yet dangerous feature of negativity-infused adaptations of the Perception Cycle — the fact that they can quickly spiral out of control and drain us of our optimism and confidence. In this battle against our leviathans, we need at least a semblance of those things, for, without them, we lose our will to push forward. Once we no longer have that, our odds of soon escaping these pernicious patterns decrease dramatically.

Yet, what makes these cycles even more difficult to break is the fact that many of us believe they start *only* with our state. In practice, that means we often wait to feel *just* right before we take action or alter our game plans, and that's not much of a strategy at all. Here's why.

First, it's not every day that our despair-filled states magically change without some kind of effort on our part; if we hang back until such changes occur, it could be a while. Second, as with all gyres, the Perception Cycle doesn't have one entry point but several. That is, we can enter at any spot and have it whip us back to where we started. I should note, however — I can't promise we won't be soaked, weathered, or more firmly in its grasp by the time we get there.

For us, what that signifies is we don't need to wait to feel less depressed before we attempt to improve our lives or current conditions. Nor do we need to sit idly by while our state slowly changes on its own — we can also cause that state to change. Moreover, by going out and trying to improve our situations, we sometimes create the same feelings for which we were previously waiting. Such emotions drive us into more empowering mental representations of the world, more effective courses of action, and more positive subsequent repetitions of the cycle.

Though it will sound a bit random or unrelated, I often try to leverage this entry-point-related feature of the process in my day-to-day experiences as an author. Specifically, knowing that I seldom *feel* ready to pen a blog post or book chapter, I don't wait for such emotions to emerge. Instead, I either force myself to start writing and let the act itself bring me a better feeling, or I go for a run, get myself in a good state, and find that, suddenly, I *want* to write. And while writing and depression are two very different subject matters, we still can, with a bit of caution, apply this same logic to our despair.

Namely, rather than waiting for our hopeless feelings to pass, we can get up off our couches, move our bodies around, and push ourselves into new, more resourceful states. Sure, sometimes those states are short-lived, but other times, they inject much-needed energy into our days and throw the Perception Cycle off course just long enough for us to alter our stories, take more inspired action, and adopt more beneficial patterns altogether.

THE DISTINCTIVE QUALITIES OF THE ABYSS

To me, the most perplexing thing about depression is how quickly we can move from a positive state to a negative one, even when our life conditions don't change all that much. I'm sure you can relate to this sort of thing. One day, you're riding high, feeling like your melancholy will never return, and the next, you're pulled back down into the abyss, begging for mercy, for seemingly no reason at all. Ah, how soon we forget. It's enough to make any of us feel foolish.

So, just why do we find ourselves falling prey to this sort of trick? It all stems back to the two most important concepts we've covered thus far — the state machine and the Perception Cycle. Specifically, when we're in happy states, we have a hard time conceptualizing the return of our depression because it's nowhere in sight. All we see are sunny skies. Moreover, not only do we feel good, but our outlooks, actions, and results look pretty great as well. We're cheersing our mates on the main deck while staring at a horizon that shows nothing but tranquil waters and inviting islands.

With depression, however, these states don't last. Instead, we spiral out of them and into more dismal ones fairly regularly. Unfortunately, with those changes in state, we also lose our ability to see what's good in the world and our compelling reasons for taking inspired action. While these fluctuations are undoubtedly challenging to deal with, we must remember they're par for the depression-laden course as well as a distinctive feature of the abyss itself.

If you've ever heard the Buddhist proverb "when the student is ready, the teacher will appear," you'll know that the logic behind it is similar to the state-based conclusions I'm putting forth here. No, it's not that our teachers magically materialize before our eyes one day; in reality, they're usually in front of us all along. It's just that we aren't always in the right state to see them and the lessons they're ready to share with us. As we change, we sometimes see those teachers in different, more edifying fashions.

As it applies to our moods and the Perception Cycle, this maxim also suggests that scary and depressing ideas don't affect us too strongly or have as much power over us when we're in the right frame of mind. In such a frame, our presence, happiness, or optimism prevents the dark soil in our psyches from becoming fertile and allowing seeds of gloom and doom to plant themselves and grow.

However, as soon as we fall into a depressive state, those same spooky concepts and possibilities penetrate the walls of our minds quite easily. Worse yet, in our most despair-filled states, such ideas appear much more real and threatening. Thus, because we're in a sorry mental frame or "ready" in such scenarios, it feels as though our teachers of gloom and doom have emerged out of thin air when, in fact, they've been there the whole time. We just weren't in the right headspace to see them.

This is why we often experience an "oh crap, here I am again" feeling when we fall back into depression. It's also why we ask how it's even possible we didn't see such a thing coming. In actuality, our negative perspectives and views of the world were there for the taking all along. They just didn't affect us much when we were feeling good — our jovial moods kept us safe from them.

The funny thing about this process is, at any time we so choose, we can jump back into our heads and replicate the same troubling feelings that define our depressive states. To put it another way, though our positive frames of mind shield us from the darkness, they don't necessarily make us impervious to it. Should we really want to regress into despair, all we'd have to do is focus on what scares or distresses us the most. But, of course, none of us would ever willingly do such a thing, right?

To keep this discussion rolling, let's return to the concept of the abyss and recall what a whirlpool actually looks like. And, no, I'm not referring to the appliance brand or the kind you step into at the gym. I'm talking about the massive, spiraling vortices in the middle of the sea — the ones that shipwreck and annihilate sailors.

If we think of depression as one of these vortices, then getting sucked into it looks a lot like being dragged underwater and forced into the grip of the current. This is a problem as it pertains to both our figurative sailing journeys and our actual lives, for if we're struggling to stay afloat, we can't tell where we're going — nor can we move in desirable directions.

When we apply this whirlpool-inspired metaphor to our real-world battles, getting pulled below the surface means we can't tap into the uplifting perspectives we did when we were in healthier, more empowering states. It also means we struggle to believe we'll escape our terrible, present conditions or get back above the waves in the future. This lack of belief, in turn, makes it harder for us to see the things that could help us do just that — the phone calls to family members, hangouts with friends, or favorite activities in which we could partake. This, once again, is state-dependent and abyss-fueled blindness — scotoma.

Unfortunately, such nearsightedness can affect more than just how we see the events and opportunities in front of us. When we're in negative versions of the Perception Cycle, our entire view of our lives can change, just as it did with participants in the 1983 study from the last chapter. In these cycles and the moods associated with them, we sometimes convince ourselves we've always been unsatisfied or depressed and always will be.

As difficult as it is to fight through such hellish experiences, we have to remember that these outlooks are products of our current states and cycles — not accurate depictions of our lives or the world. Yes, everything may look dark, even hopeless, but, eventually, these grim moods will pass, and with them, so will that hopelessness.

This is why I often say, "The problem is not the problem. The problem is the state." That is, when we're in a depressed mood, we tend to make a monster out of some idea, belief, or concern that later shrinks in size or even disappears once our mood improves. These ideas are things we'd rarely dwell on if we felt good or cheerful from the get-go. Thus, the real issue in these scenarios is that we wrestle or go to war with such state-specific problems and, in turn, sink ourselves into negative Perception Cycles for extended periods.

Unfortunately, we need to move from depression back to a more uplifting state at least once before we can truly comprehend this conundrum. Then, upon returning to healthy functioning, we can stop and say to ourselves, "Ah, I get now. It wasn't necessarily my external circumstances that changed. It was I who did the changing."

Of course, I'd be remiss if I didn't also say that there *are* times when the problem really is the problem. As such, when I recite this adage, please don't think I'm trying to downplay anything you may currently be going through. I know many folks who've been through some pretty awful circumstances, and I'm sure you do, too. You may even be one of those people.

If you are, please know you have my sympathy and prayers. That said, you also have my dedication to helping you. In the process of providing that help, I'm inevitably going to throw a lot of different ideas at you. Like this phrase, sometimes they'll stick, and, other times, they'll fall flat. I guess that's just part of the game.

So, with that admission on the table, let's cautiously return to our state-related learnings and try to tie things up. If we had to distill this chapter's discussions into one simple takeaway, it would be to remember that when it comes to states and depression, our current mood isn't always an accurate representation of our lives, our futures, or the world in general. Once we acknowledge this fact, we can more easily look past the state or cycle we're in and remind ourselves things really will get better, even if that doesn't yet seem possible.

Thankfully, however, such reassurances become much more conceivable after we've gotten through our first bout of depression. That's because, on the other side of our battle with that leviathan, we see, firsthand, that leaving our dark frame of mind is indeed feasible — just as such wisdom said it was. That alleviation of our despair serves as our lighthouse in the middle of the treacherous ocean — the thing we can set our sights on the next time we get pulled into the chasm.

Of course, it's much easier for me to sit here and make such statements than it is for any one of us to leverage these ideas amid a depressive episode. Unfortunately, I think that just comes with the territory, and, as such, I have no alternative but to ask you to trust me. Trust that I've been to some of the same depths you have. Trust that I've used these ideas to come back from such dark places. And trust that, even if you can't see it right now, things will get better. Because they definitely will.

TRIANGULAR SAILS

At the front of many pirate ships, you'll notice a set of three-sided sails. These sails are known as *the jibs*, and, like most sails, they assist with navigation and propulsion. However, since they're usually smaller than mainsails or topsails, their impact on such processes is a bit less pronounced. How they really make a name for themselves, then, is by acting as airfoils, increasing the overall stability of their vessels.[32]

Though I'd love to tell you about all the other kinds of sails on our ships as well, I'm afraid we'll only have time for this one category at the moment. After all, our goal in this book is navigating the abyss, not starting a boat supply store, and we need to stay focused on the former. As such, we'll instead dive deeper into the stabilizing, triangular sails I just introduced, for once we understand what their real-world counterparts are and how to use them, we'll be better prepared to weather our mental maelstroms.

That brings us to our current task: identifying the three-sided strategies and ideas that help us keep our own vessels stable, secure, and away from hazards. Or, to put it another, more familiar way, that means our present aim is to pinpoint the strongest influences on our internal states and figure out how we can leverage them to get ourselves out of the most momentous loops of the Perception Cycle.

TRIANGULAR SAILS

Though that may sound like an abstract chore at first, I promise we'll simplify it and make it more concrete by the end of this chapter. One of the ways we'll do that is by leaning on some of the most popular and effective tools and frameworks from the field of psychiatry. Interestingly enough, we map such ideas to the three-sided sails of our ships not just for literary effect — but also because they're three-part paradigms themselves.

THE JIB TOPSAIL

The foremost jib on our ships, the jib topsail, represents the first of these concepts: *the Cognitive Triangle* — an essential diagram that arises from a well-known, psychosocial form of mental health treatment: *Cognitive Behavioral Therapy*.[33] In their practices, doctors use this drawing to help patients make connections between three event-specific phenomena: their thoughts in response to the incident in question, their resulting feelings, and, finally, their subsequent behaviors. Clinicians aren't the only ones who get to leverage this tool, however. We can take advantage of it as well once we fully understand what it is.

When we listen to the Cognitive Triangle's teachings, we learn that our thoughts surrounding any event play a significant role in determining how we feel about it. Those feelings then direct what actions we will or won't take in response to such an occurrence. Or, in simpler terms, what we think strongly affects how we feel, and how we feel influences how we act.

If this all sounds a bit reminiscent of the Perception Cycle, then I have to commend you for following along so closely. In reality, these concepts are pretty similar, aside from two finer details. The first is that the Cognitive Triangle focuses mainly on the thoughts a particular stimulus elicits in our minds, while the Perception Cycle explores how our current state influences our interpretation of not only *that* stimulus but, possibly, many other similarly-timed ones as well. The second is that, because of what I just mentioned, the Cognitive Triangle is the superior framework for analyzing and predicting specific and finite actions, whereas the Perception Cycle is the better tool for making sense of more complex, prolonged, or recurring circumstances.

As it pertains to depression, the Cognitive Triangle suggests that when something negative happens in our lives, if we react to that event with helpless and hopeless thoughts, we'll likely feel melancholic. As a result, we'll do things a melancholic person would. For example, let's say we get fired from our jobs and immediately think two things: that our termination was our fault and that we'll never find another position. In telling ourselves such stories, we'll not only experience a good amount of grief, but we'll also likely obstruct ourselves from applying to new jobs until that grief subsides.

Now, the interesting thing about these kinds of scenarios, and one of the main lessons the Cognitive Triangle seeks to teach us, is that we sometimes interpret what unfolds around us incorrectly. For example, maybe it wasn't our fault we got fired.

Perhaps our company just needed to make some painful layoffs after its biggest client went out of business unexpectedly.

When we latch onto more uplifting conclusions such as this one, we not only use the Triangle to our advantage, but we also make ourselves feel better about our situations. Yet, we need not stop there, either. We can also take this style of thinking one level higher to reveal another of the Triangle's fundamental teachings.

That idea is that, regardless of what happens to us, we decide how to evaluate and make sense of said occurrences. When we misperceive challenging yet manageable ones — be it because we hold some disempowering belief or cognitive bias — we cause our undesirable feelings to grow and inhibit ourselves from taking inspired action.

Now, of course, not all our troubles in life fall into that *manageable* category. Nor am I trying to suggest such a thing with this discussion. All I'm attempting to do is remind us that, in many perturbing situations, such as when we wreck our cars or lose a prized possession, we still have a critical choice to make. That choice is to either see these events as reasons to let the abyss consume us once more or view them as learning opportunities and reminders of some of our better fortunes.

And while it may sound like I'm being overly optimistic or approaching tribulation with a Pollyanna-like mindset, consider this. Every interpretation we make is either helpful or harmful. Since we choose how we see the events in our lives, we also choose our reactions and their overall constructiveness. That's why, when it comes to leveraging this first figurative sail and finding stability amid chaos, we have to be very careful with what we say to ourselves.

Right or wrong, our self-talk guides our feelings and behaviors. If we want to avoid the abyss, we must deliberately modify our internal chatter so that it's beneficial for us, even if it seems slightly out of touch or foolish. We must adjust our jib topsail by remembering that, although bad things sometimes happen, we can usually lessen their effect on us if we leverage the first point of the Cognitive Triangle properly. The sooner we do that — and I realize how difficult that can be in the face of depression — the sooner we'll get back to sailing toward our next port.

THE JIB

Though it certainly doesn't strike inspiration into the heart of anyone who hears it, the name for our second jib is just the plain old *jib*. But don't blame me — I don't make the rules around here. I just come up with the contrived and overused metaphors.

To connect this second sail to another well-known mental health framework, I have to introduce you to the father of Cognitive Therapy, Aaron T. Beck.[34] In the industry, Beck is known for a wide array of accomplishments and discoveries, including the creation of his *Depression Inventory* — a tool for measuring the disorder — also known as the BDI.[35] With this invention, Beck altered the ways many mental health professionals view the disease.

At the time of its unveiling in 1961, countless experts thought depression emanated mainly due to conflicts between our conscious and unconscious motivations.[36] However, Beck flipped that notion on its head and showed us just how important our thoughts and beliefs are in our experience of the dreaded affliction.

After putting forth his groundbreaking BDI, Beck created yet another game-changing framework for looking at and evaluating the condition. This second framework — his *Cognitive Triad* — is what our current jib will represent. With this tool, also known as *the Negative Triad*, Beck suggested that what contributes most to our experience of depression are disempowering beliefs.[37] And not just any old beliefs — you guessed it — three specific types in particular. Those three categories, as Beck outlined, are beliefs about ourselves, our world, and our futures. When we buy into harmful and pervasive ideas in each sector, we set ourselves up for gloom, doom, and despair.

For example, we may tell ourselves we're worthless, that the world is a terrible and evil place, and that none of these things will ever change. I don't think I even need to describe what such ideas will do to our psyches. These are pessimistic viewpoints of the highest order, and we should take immense caution before subscribing to them.

Though it doesn't take a rocket scientist to see the toxicity of such ideas, there's still a crucial, hidden takeaway underlying them that we must not overlook — one that relates to Beck's original unveiling of his BDI. Specifically, while a far greater percentage of people today acknowledge the power of our thoughts and beliefs in our experience of depression than in 1961, few of us still ever evaluate or attempt to change what we think and believe. I mean, seriously, how many of us who feel life is unfair or that we're worthless pause to question such notions and how we came to accept them? Not too many, I'd argue.

And while the intense feelings that arise from such ideas sometimes stop us in our tracks and prevent us from shifting them so easily, when it comes to leveraging our second jib, we must still attempt to make such changes, regardless of the difficulty. We must step back and ask ourselves the tough personal questions, such as, "Do I really think I'm unlovable or incapable of achieving what I want in life?" More importantly, if we don't like our answers to those questions, we must do our best to eradicate the disempowering beliefs behind them and replace them with more hopeful, uplifting ones. Otherwise, we run the risk of facing intense mental hardship or sailing straight into the maelstrom.

Of course, attacking and changing our thoughts and beliefs might not always occur overnight. However, that's not a valid reason for abandoning such tasks altogether. After all, I'm sure you remember the concept we discussed called learned helplessness; well, to give up on trying to shift our beliefs simply because it's difficult is just another form of it. Yes, replacing harmful ideas we've accepted for years will be challenging, and yes, it will take time, but with enough patience and persistence, we can make it happen.

If we want to avoid our sea serpents, we have to fight these feelings of helplessness as early and as often as possible. This is depression, after all. It's a battle for our souls and minds. One way or another, it's going to take discipline and dedication. Until we start subscribing to the correct beliefs about ourselves, our world, and our futures, those unwanted creatures will continue encroaching on the sacred territory of our psyches.

THE STAYSAIL

To round out our jib-related discussions, let's finally talk about the last of them — the staysail. Now, if we want to get into semantics, ships can, and often do, have more than one of these. That's because, in general, the word *staysail* refers to any triangular sail that runs lengthwise along its ship's hull.

So, while all three of our jibs are technically staysails, our focus is on the innermost of them, the one commonly referred to as *the* staysail. Like the previous jibs we covered, this one helps us stabilize our vessels and make them more aerodynamic. It also represents yet another three-sided depression framework I want to discuss — something I call *the Negativity Timeline*.

This new framework piggybacks off the third side of Beck's Cognitive Triad — the one suggesting that pessimistic beliefs about our futures leave us vulnerable to depression. Specifically, it dictates that when we perceive our past, present, and future as bleak or hopeless, we'll inevitably experience some form of despair. That notion applies even if our other triad-related beliefs — those about ourselves and our world — are positive.

Think about it this way. Most of us have been through trials and tribulations in the past. We've lost loved ones, failed in essential areas of our lives, and faced rejections from employers and potential mates. And yet, many of us have also managed to overcome these challenges and find prosperity anyway. Such triumphs show us that our pasts don't always dictate our futures and that our hardships can sometimes be the very things that propel us to success later in life.

However, those same hardships *can* determine our futures if we let them. This is especially the case when we cling to them or assume that, because we've experienced loss and depression in the past, we'll always fall prey to similar, unfortunate circumstances. Though such assumptions can be overwhelming at times, they simply aren't true. Yes, moving forward in life is often quite trying, especially when we're healing from trauma or tragedy. But the mere presence of such misfortunes doesn't mean we'll never escape them. We must not forget that.

When we do, we color our lives in negativity. We see the past, present, and future in a dismal light and tell ourselves we shouldn't even try to make things better. This perspective invites helplessness and hopelessness — the driving forces behind depression — toward us once more. When these emotions permeate our entire life's timeline, they overwhelm us and rob us of our will to press on.

That's why, when guiding our ships through the most troubled waters, we have to remember that no matter how terrible we currently feel, such emotions will eventually dissipate. Sure, weathering our present storm might take a while or be extremely difficult. But if we lean on our staysails by remembering that every squall eventually passes, we'll find the energy we need to keep sailing.

In time, that energy will allow us to not only let go of the Negativity Timeline but also rediscover our guiding light in the dark sea: hope. That uplifting force helps us navigate back to shore by illuminating the safest routes and tactics. With more of those tactics at our disposal, we give ourselves a better chance of avoiding the menacing vortex in the distance.

SCYLLA, MEET CHARYBDIS

In Greek mythology, Homer introduced us to two of the scariest creatures ever to inhabit the ocean: Scylla and Charybdis. These leviathans sat on either side of the Strait of Messina, the body of water between Sicily and mainland Italy. The first of the two materialized as a six-headed, cliff-dwelling colossus, while the second took the shape of a whirlpool created by a rarely seen, subaquatic beast.

This pair posed such a threat to passing ships that few crews ever dared to venture through the strait. Both monsters were so powerful that coming in contact with either one, more often than not, would end in catastrophe. Moreover, the section of the strait where these two horrors lived was quite narrow, so avoiding one typically meant getting too close to the other. Consequently, and as the saying goes, those sailing through this thin passageway often found themselves *stuck between Scylla and Charybdis.*

When it comes to mental health, we face our own versions of these two behemoths: anxiety and depression. The former manifests much like Scylla — a fear-inducing, terrifying opponent that leaves us shaken to our core, while the latter incarnates as none other than a Charybdis-like abyss — a never-ending, downward spiral that pulls us in and pushes us to the brink of shipwreck.

SCYLLA, MEET CHARYBDIS

Just like this pair of oceanic beasts, each of our mental health monsters can lead us to the other. In fact, according to the research, that appears to be the rule with these disorders — not the exception.[38] As such, like sailors in the Strait of Messina, we often get too close to Scylla, try to course-correct, and end up in the grasp of Charybdis' whirlpool. Though this process can be, and often is, terrifying, there is a way out of the madness: We can decide not to sail near Scylla in the first place. We can learn to chart our course around Sicily and navigate to whichever safe Italian village we desire.

FROM ANXIETY TO DEPRESSION

In 2015, a group of researchers at West Virginia University conducted a study to determine how rodents respond to unpredictable, chronic, and mild stressors — a process known as the UCMS protocol.[39] In that study, Dr. Jefferson Frisbee and his team exposed several mice to various environmental aggravations by wetting their sleeping quarters, removing their beds, titling their cages, and manipulating their sleep-wake cycles.

When Frisbee's mice first encountered these stressors, they went into fight-flight-or-freeze mode. They scampered around anxiously and looked for ways to escape said stimuli. However, as the experiment wore on, they became less prone to frantically seek safety. Instead, they primarily sat motionless and miserable, exhibiting melancholy-like symptoms and anhedonia — the inability to feel pleasure. These results not only reinforced previous findings surrounding the UCMS protocol's depression-evoking efficacy but also popularized its process and lastingly associated Frisbee's team with it.

In many ways, this experiment wasn't all that different from one we previously discussed — that of Martin Seligman and his dogs. Both studies show us that when we place any organism in a fear-inducing environment, it will, at first, do its best to run from or fight with the stressors placed upon it. However, if that organism can't remove or avoid such stressors in a reasonable amount of time, it'll soon lose hope that such a thing is even possible.[40] This is the mindset of learned helplessness. What often starts as terror and anxiety eventually becomes detachedness and depression.

Though Frisbee's team's research was similar to Seligman's in that it revolved around stress and animals, it differed slightly in its conclusions. The first of those conclusions was the notion with which we opened this chapter — anxiety can, and often does, lead to depression. The second was that our environments are one of the primary sources of stress in our lives.

Both of these conclusions are particularly interesting for us because they speak to the importance of the social sphere of our biopsychosocial model. That is, they show us what psychologist Tirril Harris and her co-author George Brown told us in their 1978 book, *The Social Origins of Depression*. Namely, it's not just our brain chemistry and thoughts that contribute to our experience of the disease — it's also our external worlds and the myriad of other factors that fall under our *social* umbrella.[41]

But still, what does all this research mean for us in terms of avoiding mental illness? Good question. Primarily, it suggests that no matter how we think or use our bodies, if our environments are continually bringing us mild and unpredictable stress, at some point, we'll likely encounter anxiety — possibly even depression. Thus, even though we've focused on the biological and psychological realms throughout this book thus far, we'd be remiss if we didn't also take the time to analyze and reconfigure our surroundings in a way that removes any sources of undue strain.

Now, I know what you might be thinking: Few of us regularly face the same stressors as Frisbee's mice, so why would we have to worry about such a thing? The answer, somewhat surprisingly, has less to do with *specific* stressors than the frequency and intensity of them. After all, it's called the unpredictable, chronic, mild stress protocol — not the "remove the bed method." In other words, the ways we could experience said stress are unspecified, and therefore, virtually limitless.

Okay, so that's all well and good, but if we actually encounter the UCMS protocol in our daily lives, where's all that stress coming from? We live in the most prosperous, technologically advanced, data-driven times in history. There's no way our modern lifestyles could be contributing to the amount of strain we endure daily, right? Unfortunately, I think you know the answer to that question already.

THE NEW SOURCES OF STRESS

Let's face it. Life today is challenging. That's not to say it wasn't in the past, just that it's different than it used to be. Now, don't get me wrong. I'd much rather live in our modern world than the disease and war-plagued dark ages. At the same time, however, I can't deny how stressful our always-on, fast-paced society can sometimes be.

Two of the primary sources of that stress are our ubiquitous smart devices and toxic media outlets. Our phones, computers, and notifications follow us everywhere we go. With them, they bring constant fun and entertainment as well as gloom and doom. I say "constant" because one of the only times we're without them is when we're asleep. And even then, as soon as we wake, we roll over and check our texts, email, and social media once more.

Naturally, there are many reasons we do such a thing. One is that it's a habit we've conditioned ourselves into over the years. Another is that it's exciting to stay up to date and connected. When we're online, we can chat with friends, work on our businesses, and read the latest rumors about our favorite sports teams. But that's not all we can do. We can also stumble upon some serious stress and negativity.

For example, we might find angry emails from our biggest clients, unsettling memos from our physicians, and breaking news articles warning how another world war is all but imminent. These notifications and stories are enough to make anyone go mad, and many of them appear prior to us pouring our first cup of coffee.

Of course, I'm exaggerating slightly. It's not *every* morning our feeds and notifications are overly and utterly negative. It's just that they're always, well, *there*, waiting to deliver the next update. Decades ago, when horrific things happened across the globe, we wouldn't learn about them for days. Sometimes, we wouldn't hear about them at all. Now, those same terrible occurrences immediately plant themselves in our social media timelines and try to put us in fight-flight-or-freeze mode the moment we arise from our slumber.

Yet, even after we've fully awoken and taken our first bites of breakfast, the stress of our days often continues to grow. As we commute to work or school or simply take a break in whatever it is we're doing, we usually glance at our devices. On them, we see troubling headlines, internet personalities with perfect bodies, and ads from a slew of companies suggesting that if we don't buy their latest, hottest products, we'll fall behind and lose touch with our peers.

Worse yet, for those of us at the office, instant messages, group chats, company-wide announcements, and calendar invites bombard us from the minute we sit down at our desks. Moreover, productivity-related software programs constantly remind us we're below quota or behind on our deadlines and that the companies down the street, heck, even the firms overseas and robots in Silicon Valley, are trying to take our lunch. And that's assuming we're full-time employees. If we're contractors — which more of us are becoming these days thanks to our gig-based economy —

we have the added pressure of always being on the lookout for our next assignment. How fun.

If we're not careful, all these sources of stress and comparison can infiltrate every part of our lives and lead to a great deal of uncertainty and anxiety. When we add enough of them together, we create routines and environments that propagate burnout and depression at an astonishing pace. As such, we must be meticulous with what we let appear on our screens, in our timelines, and through our minds at *all* hours — not just those revolving around breakfast or where we spend the majority of our weekdays.

Though this may sound a bit out of left field, the sum of these current-day strains and fears makes me not at all surprised to hear that marijuana is now legal in more than fifteen US states. With life as demanding and disquieting as ever, many folks are desperate for new ways to unwind and temporarily forget their worldly stressors. Over the years, as more people experimented with the drug and found it to be somewhat safe and a reliable relaxation tool, it became only a matter of time before citizens brought their findings to local representatives and attempted to reshape public policy.

One thing such a societal and legal change reflects is that, despite past promises that advances in technology would make our lives easier and less hectic, in many ways, they've done the opposite. In the 1930s, economists like John Maynard Keynes suggested such advances would save us great deals of time and effort in our homes and workplaces.[42] In turn, we'd be able to drastically cut back on labor-related hours and dedicate more of them to family, leisure, and passion-filled pursuits.

Instead, in the last few decades, we've jumped into a technological arms race with companies and countries all around the globe. As a result, we still work just as long, but now we have less job security and are too afraid to slow down. After all, if we do, the largest players in our field might replicate our companies' offerings overnight and put us out of commission.

Though most of us handle these pervasive threats and work-related stressors gracefully at first, over time, enough projects, deadlines, meetings, and industry developments can stack up and push us to the brink of overwhelm and anxiety. Sometimes, we can escape or evade such negative feelings with a weekend off or a relaxing vacation. However, if, after countless holidays, we find that our jobs still haven't slowed down at all, our risk of burnout and despair increases dramatically.

In these situations, we see our never-ending mountains of assignments and think, "These tasks keep accumulating. The notifications never stop. What's the point of even trying to keep up?" And so, just like mice exposed to the UCMS protocol, we resign ourselves to our persistent stressors and fall back into depressed states. This doesn't exactly help us, but sometimes, it feels like the only option in our modern, frenetic lives.

A DISEASE OF MODERNITY

In my last book, the first entry in the *Get Out of Your Head* series, I argued anxiety is an offshoot of an evolutionarily preserved survival mechanism. Here's what I meant by that. Those of our ancestors who were both sensitive to predatory threats and fast or smart enough to avoid them stood the best chance of living long enough to pass their genes to offspring; with that passing came the transfer of their vigilant fight-flight-or-freeze inclinations.

Over time, and thanks to innovations in technology, security, and agriculture, our world became far less dangerous than it once was. Now, we no longer come across as many ferocious animals or life-threatening situations as our survivalist ancestors. However, the fear centers of our brains are still operating as if that's the case. As such, they remain as active and alert as ever. This discrepancy between their default sense of vigilance and the relative safety of our world today is one of the main reasons anxiety runs rampant in our society.[43]

It's fairly easy to find examples that illustrate the sort of thing I'm talking about here. Namely, during challenging conversations, job interviews, and first dates, it's not uncommon for our hearts to race out of our chests or our palms to sweat uncontrollably. Evolutionarily speaking, such things occur because our brains equate these relatively new sources of uncertainty with some of the life-or-death situations our predator-evading ancestors faced long ago.

Back then, when we lived in small tribes, attempting to make a new friend or court a potential mate required risking a severe form of rejection. Not just from the person we were approaching but also from the group itself. For our predecessors, that prospective ostracization would mean having to go it alone in the wild — a fate very few survived. Thus, as a species, we quickly learned, both through real-life experiences and the process of natural selection, to think twice about doing anything that might result in such a devastating outcome.[44]

Today, however, bombing an interview isn't nearly as dangerous as the social equivalent from fifty thousand years ago. When such an unfortunate event transpires in present times, all we have to do is get on a job-posting website to find ourselves another opportunity. Yet even though we know this on a fundamental level, we still often react to such circumstances as if global social acceptance were actually on the line. Just why is that?

The reason is that we're still mainly working with the same brain, and all its hardwired survival instincts, as that of our exile-wary ancestors. Sure, it may sound crazy, but the truth is, evolution occurs fairly slowly, at least in comparison to the pace at which culture and technology progress. According to scientists, our brains likely haven't evolved in 30,000 to 100,000 years.[45] And, yet, in just the last one hundred or so, we've seen commercial airliners take flight, men walk on the moon, scientists sequence the human genome, digital innovations disrupt almost every industry on the planet, and so on.

All these breakthroughs, and many more, have recently and radically altered how we live and work, and, yet, our brains haven't changed in at least three hundred of those one-hundred-year periods. What that means for us is many of the things we do today don't necessarily jibe with the way our bodies were built, and that discrepancy often brings us great distress. In other words, we can still get super nervous when walking into an interview, even if performing poorly during it won't affect our long-term social or survival prospects.

When it comes to depression, I'd argue that the same evolutionary concept applies. Specifically, according to the research, depression is, to a large degree, a disease of the modern lifestyle.[46] Of course, that's not to say it's *only* a disease of modernity, just that the fashion in which we currently live has a significant impact on its prevalence worldwide. If not for many of the obvious ills of our society, such as isolation, improper diet, inactivity, advanced warfare, and the destruction of our planet, we wouldn't see nearly as much despair as we do today.

To comprehend the effect that lifestyle has on overarching rates of mental illness, all we have to do is look at communities that have yet to adopt a thoroughly modern way of life. Luckily, researchers have made that task pretty easy for us.

For example, in 1976, psychiatrist Abram Hostetter set out to determine the rate of mood disorders amongst members of the Amish community.[47] His findings? Of the 12,500 people surveyed, only 112 exhibited active symptoms of mental illness, a rate twenty-two times lower than that of society at large today: one in five people.[48] Of course, the world has changed a great deal since 1976, yet, still, a mental illness rate of less than one percent in any population was, and still is, virtually unheard of outside of Hostetter's study.

Another group of depression-dodging people that researchers have followed closely is the Kaluli tribe of hunter-gatherers in Papua New Guinea. These folks live a lifestyle pretty close to that of our remote ancestors. They get plenty of sunlight and exercise, have close bonds with tribe members, and eat natural, unprocessed foods. As a result, they experience almost zero cases of mental illness annually.[49]

So, what is it that makes these communities relatively impervious to melancholy? To put it simply: they avoid most, if not all, of the mental-illness-promoting habits associated with our contemporary lifestyles. They eschew isolation, restlessness, nutrient-deprived foods, and sedentariness. They also evade stress-inducing push notifications, alerts, and other digital beckoners of our attention.

When you seriously consider these insights, it might appear as though the human body just wasn't meant for our frantic, modern way of life. And while that's certainly true in some regards, I don't think it paints the whole picture. Nor does it help us all that much.

After all, we can't forget the fantastic things our speedy society also provides us — for example, central heating and air conditioning, endless supplies of food, and days' worth of knowledge and entertainment at our fingertips. I'm sure none of us would want to get rid of these modern marvels. Nor should we have to.

What it seems we need to do, though, is find a way to balance our ancestors' lifestyles with our own. In doing so, we'll take the best of each and use it to create a personalized mental health playbook — one that harnesses the upside and more readily helps us avoid the downside. Though we've been developing that playbook throughout our time together, we'll keep penning its figurative pages in the forthcoming chapters. For now, however, let's continue our discussion by looking into one of the most common side-effects of our modern lives — isolation.

LONELINESS: A PRECURSOR TO DEPRESSION

In the new, digital age, we tend to say we're more connected than ever before. However, on the other side of that idea lies an opposing piece of wisdom: Despite our digital connectedness, we've never been further apart from one another. When put together, these two contradictory ideas compose what's known as the Social Media Paradox.[50]

This paradox tells us that, regardless of how many friends and followers we have online, the surface-level interactions they promote either can't or don't replace the in-depth ones our bodies crave. Moreover, it suggests the constant checking of our phones and laptops for likes, notifications, updates, and messages often gets in the way of those more important, authentic connections. After all, it's hard to have a deep, in-person conversation if we can't pick our heads up from our devices.

Of course, that's not to say all forms of digital interaction are bad for us. In fact, countless journal articles and research studies have disproven such a notion.[51] It's just the quick, superficial, hostile, or inauthentic ones that prove harmful. These are the same ones social media tends to foster.[52]

When we confuse these more shallow interactions for the deep, genuine ones we need, we make ourselves vulnerable to isolation and loneliness — two well-known precursors to depression.[53] That is, we allow such exchanges to convince us we've checked our proverbial boxes for socializing and connecting each day. In reality, our bodies know we haven't and send us all sorts of warning signals as a result, such as insomnia, a disregard for external threats to our well-being, and heightened senses of defensiveness and hopelessness.[54] The only problem is, we're usually too stressed out and distracted to notice them.

Our increasingly urban-centric lifestyles only further exacerbate this problem. If you've ever lived or worked in the city, you'll know what I'm talking about. Every day, we're surrounded by countless strangers — on the commute to work, in our office buildings, and at our favorite lunch spots. These crowded situations — particularly those where we don't actually talk to anyone — can make us think we're the last folks on Earth who need to worry about seclusion. However, they can also be just as misleading as social media in terms of hitting our daily connection quotas.

Though our conscious minds may recall these stranger-filled scenarios and say, "I haven't been isolated recently! I've been around people all week!" our subconscious minds know better. After all, isolation is about *feeling* distant from others — not physically *being* away from them. Without sustained doses of that necessary emotional component, our bodies go into self-preservation mode, bombarding us with the same sorts of warning signals outlined just a moment ago.

These signals are something renowned neuroscientist John Cacioppo researched throughout his career. In his book, *Loneliness: Human Nature and the Need for Social Connection*, as well as several studies he conducted, Cacioppo sought to answer an important question: "What exactly takes place in our bodies when we're isolated?"[55]

In one of those studies, he tapped a group of Chicago residents to prove that loneliness leads to elevated blood pressure, sleep disruptions, and a reduced ability to fight disease.[56] In a later trial, two of Cacioppo's followers, Leah Doane and Emma Adam, set out to build upon that experiment as well as Cacioppo's overall findings on seclusion.[57]

They started by programming a set of smartwatch-like gadgets to beep regularly over three consecutive days, then affixed the devices to participants' wrists to monitor their activity and sleep-wake cycles. When the watches sounded, subjects would collect saliva samples and answer questions about their moods.

At the end of the experiment, the pair drew some rather astonishing conclusions from the data they collected. One of the things they found was that participants' levels of the stress hormone cortisol spiked whenever they reported feeling lonely.

Moreover, those who experienced such a feeling at any time during the trial exhibited changes to their regular cortisol cycles — the ones that typically follow our circadian rhythms.

When all three scientists combined their findings with the prevailing loneliness literature, they deduced that our bodies approach solitude just like they would real, physical threats.[58] They release stress hormones, pump blood to our extremities, and prepare us to take action. This preparation is another helpful feature of our evolutionarily conditioned survival instincts. There is one problem with it, however, and it's that there's a difference between *preparing* us to take action and *making* us do so.

What that means for our battles with depression is, since most of us are just trying to keep our heads and vessels above water, such bodily signals aren't always enough to distract us from our despair. In fact, sometimes, they only debilitate us further. As such, we often remain in negative renditions of the Perception Cycle, unconvinced that taking loneliness-fighting action might improve our mood or relieve us of some of the stress we're experiencing. This inaction keeps us stuck in our isolation — a condition reportedly as dangerous to our health as smoking — and beckons our leviathans toward our boats once more.[59]

THE CYCLICAL NATURE OF MENTAL HEALTH

So I think we've set the scene properly. We've talked about how perpetual, unpredictable stress, including isolation, often leads to anxiety and how anxiety can sometimes lead to depression. But what we haven't yet fleshed out is how that process can also become a vicious cycle — one that traps us between our two dreaded sea monsters, Scylla and Charybdis.

And while not all mental health battles take the same form, many of them, especially in today's tech-driven world, follow this particular path. That is, we encounter any number of erratic stressors in our environment, such as seclusion and device-driven panic, and fall into states of fear and overwhelm.

At the first sign of these feelings, we tend to pull ourselves out of society even further. That way, others won't see that we're struggling. Unfortunately, such a strategy rarely benefits us. Namely, rather than providing an opportunity for us to reset and regain our balance, it prevents us from making the authentic connections required for escaping our misery. Moreover, it gives us endless time to fixate and go deep in our heads with fears and doubts — the last place we want to be if we wish to get back to mental and emotional equilibrium.

In these situations, we sometimes find ourselves cycling from one negative mental state to another — from stressed to anxious to lonely to depressed.[60] Worse yet, that cycle often repeats itself. For example, our depression weighs us down and intensifies our hopelessness, which pushes us to hide our pain from others once again. When we do that, we experience even more anxiety and depression, and the process starts back up as if we'd sailed right into the Strait of Messina.

Yet, regardless of how terrible that process may make us feel, we must remember we likely won't return to our usual selves until we consciously end our seclusion. The same goes for stopping our obsessive, looping thinking; despite how addicting rumination can be, it's nearly impossible to think through anxiety and depression. Sure, there are some practical approaches we can apply to our worries, but there is no "solving" either condition. As the name of this book series suggests, we must instead put down our contemplations and get back out into the world.

One of the reasons behind such logic is that good feelings rarely arise from thought alone. Instead, they emerge from connecting with ourselves and others, being present and spontaneous, and engaging in activities we find fun and meaningful. Or, to echo the words of Stuart Brown, founder of the *National Institute for Play*, escaping our despair requires such things because the opposite of play isn't work — it's depression.[61] Thus, it's no wonder we feel so terrible when we're stuck in a downward spiral. We're not doing much besides isolating and overanalyzing. And we're sure as heck not playing.

When it comes to our own forms of depression-beating leisure, we can toss a baseball around with our roommates or children, try out a new board game, or attend a concert with our friends. Though these activities will seem futile during our darkest days, we should still try to partake in them anyway because they give us a glimpse into a world we disconnected from long ago — one where our worries are no longer our sole focus.

Lucky for us, these same pursuits can help flip the downward spiral upon itself, creating a feel-good cycle that makes us want to stay active or hang out with friends again in the near future. It's these opportunities we must embrace and seek more of, for they're our tickets out of our heads and misery and our escape from the harrowing Strait of Messina and the grips of Scylla and her chasm-like counterpart.

ALL ROUTES LEAD TO THE ABYSS

It's almost impossible these days to go more than ten minutes without something trying to steal our attention. In this new digital age, our phones, computers, and smartwatches constantly chime as they notify us of incoming texts, emails, likes, and updates. Though some of these messages are beneficial or necessary, many of them are not. When we let the most frightening of them invade our minds over and over again, we risk putting ourselves in ruinous, high-stress states that end in burnout and depression.

Worse yet, the most negative of these communications often come from places we couldn't possibly predict. For example, though we can easily avoid horrifying news alerts by changing the notification settings on our devices, it's much harder to protect ourselves from random, anxiety-inducing social media shares from old friends. Such posts take us by surprise, remind us of our biggest worries, and sink us below choppy waters.

That sinking is what I'm referring to when I say *all routes lead to the abyss* — any course on which we sail our ships can send us back to the vortex of depression, so long as we've let our guard down or fallen into a disempowering state. As such, and since destructive influences on our frames of mind lurk around every corner, we must be extremely cautious with where we place our focus.

ALL ROUTES LEAD TO THE ABYSS

To take this concept out of the abstract, let's look at an example. But first, to lay the groundwork for it, I must make a heavy confession. Though it likely won't come as a surprise given our previous conversations, the story I tell next won't make sense without it. So, here goes: I've always been terrified of death. Its seeming permanence and unclear meaning have haunted me most of my life; thinking about it is one of the main things that reactivates my depression and sends me into a helpless state for days, weeks, or, sometimes, months on end.

In 2019, three nights before the last episode of the popular TV series *Game of Thrones* aired, my death-related depression was as far from my mind as it had been in weeks. As I aimlessly surfed the web that night, I stumbled upon a *TechCrunch* headline suggesting the show's final season had not lived up to expectations, and therefore, should be remade entirely. Feeling similarly about that concluding season, I clicked into the article, curious to see what its author had to say.

As I waited for it to load, I had no idea what to expect. Maybe a laugh, an interesting perspective, or a potential plot twist? Though it certainly could've provided any of those things in the end, I never got far enough to find out. I only read one line before it beckoned my own version of Charybdis once more.

That line began with a popular *Game of Thrones* quote: "The night is dark and full of terrors." Then it followed up the well-known phrase with its own conclusion: "And this life is, likely, ultimately meaningless." Now I know it may sound overdramatic, but when I read those words, I was devastated.

Their nihilistic message petrified me, put me in fight-flight-or-freeze mode, and caused me to question everything I knew about life and death once more. That questioning then triggered my depression and left me reeling and fixating for the next two weeks.

Just like the rest of my bouts, that fortnight-length one was difficult to get through. However, what made it different from the others was that it led me to an important lesson and inspired me to write this chapter. That lesson tells us the following: Once we know what our triggers for depression are, we have to be very careful that we don't, intentionally or unintentionally, stumble across them in our daily lives. We must be cautious with the content we consume, the thoughts we think, and the people with whom we hang. Otherwise, sooner or later, our environments will get the best of us, and the maelstrom will re-emerge.

BE CAREFUL WHAT YOU *LOOK* FOR

Never before in human history have we had access to an endless supply of information — and in our pockets, nonetheless. Thanks to the internet and our smartphones, we can now find last night's winning lottery numbers, fetch directions to our dinner reservations, or sign a business contract from the road, all within a matter of seconds.

While these new treasure troves of data and internet-enabled eases have generally made our lives more efficient and enjoyable, they've also brought about some unintended and adverse side effects. One of the most harmful of them is that disturbing and contradictory information now hangs over us all the time. What that means, in more practical terms, is that finding viewpoints undermining almost any opinion, belief, or theory we hold takes but a few clicks or keystrokes these days. And that, more often than not, isn't so great for our mental health.

To illustrate what I'm talking about here, let's jump into another example. But first, just like last time, I need to make a semi-familiar and heavy confession: Climate change is another topic that triggers my depression. The notion that we, as humans, could not only spell our own demise but also destroy life for all generations to follow — I mean, that's just incomprehensible.

Though that admission may sound random, it relates to the subject at hand in the following fashion: If you google something akin to "climate change emergency," you'll find millions of results detailing just how grim the current crisis and outlook are. However, if you instead search "climate change isn't real," you'll discover countless pieces describing what a hoax the entire predicament is.

Now, before I go any further, I have to mention that proving or disproving the theory of climate change or any other massive, scary possibility is not my aim here. Though I *will* spend quite a bit of time talking about planetary warming in this book, that discussion is more a canvas on which to paint my ideas and strategies than it is an attempt to convince you of the current state of the world. And, for the present moment, the main idea I'm trying to get across through that discussion is that no matter what concepts or hypotheses you want to find, reinforce, or prove — accurate or not — they're out there somewhere. All you have to do is go looking for them.

The reason this is such an important, depression-related distinction to make stems back to the first triangular sail on our ships. Specifically, since negative thinking summons our melancholy, and the information we discover online can push us into misery-inducing thought patterns, then by simply researching unnerving ideas, we're unintentionally inviting despair back into our lives — regardless of the accuracy of such information. That logic applies no matter the subject of our fear-laced inquiry — the rise of artificial intelligence, the afterlife, biological warfare — the list is endless.

Unfortunately for us, the further we peek into any one of those gloom and doom topics, the harder it is to stop fixating on it. At the top, the whirlpool spins slowly, yet with each subsequent downward-dragging revolution, its circles get tighter and faster.

In practice, this abstract notion might materialize like the following. Let's say you're slightly curious about one of the subjects I just alluded to — the potential applications of artificial intelligence — and decide to research it a bit. At first, you simply peruse a few articles, looking for something interesting or eye-catching. Yet, with each additional paragraph you read, you get sucked in further and further.

Within minutes, you go from feeling slightly uneasy over the possibility of AI displacing workers to plunging down the *Terminator* rabbit hole. Worse yet, you remain in that bleak state until you decide to take a walk and clear your head — almost an hour later. Luckily, it provides the relief you desperately need and allows you to get back to your day, albeit after you'd already put yourself through a good deal of grief.

And though this quick, frustrating story is just a fictitious example, it epitomizes the real-world application of *all routes leading to the abyss* and illustrates that insidious structure's force and power. Moreover, and more importantly, it highlights why we need to be so careful with the thoughts and opinions we put into our minds. If we aren't, it's into the vortex we go.

INTENTIONAL IGNORANCE

When we're wrestling with life's gloomiest questions, it usually isn't long before we pummel ourselves, mentally, into a state of panicked obsessiveness. That state pushes us to get to the bottom of the issue or subject responsible for our despair. Much as is the case with anxiety, however, we can't "solve" these black hole matters, no matter how hard we try. The further we dive into them, the deeper and darker they get.

Yet, the reason we attempt such a thing anyway is that, when we're depressed, we aren't thinking clearly. We have blinders on and feel like nothing else exists besides what's in our direct line of sight. Typically, what's in that line is something so big and terrifying that, even if we *could* see around it, it would still petrify and immobilize us. Regardless of that fact, however, there *is* a way past these immense concerns, and it's adopting a new mindset and becoming *intentionally ignorant* of them. The following discussion explains just what that means.

If you look up the definition of the word *bliss*, you'll find something rather interesting. Though most of us realize it's a synonym for happiness, not all of us know its more intricate details. Specifically, according to the dictionary, when we're in blissful states, we're typically oblivious to everything else going on around us. That means, any time we're experiencing this uplifting emotion, we're ignoring countless negative thoughts, ideas, and stories playing out in our minds and worlds. More importantly, it means the opposite is also true — when we're depressed, we're usually hyperfocusing on some of those same undesirable thoughts and subjects.

Just as we can't be blissful without some level of ignorance on our part, we can't move out of our melancholic states without a touch of that same psychological force. This is something author Andrew Solomon reminds us of in *The Noonday Demon*, one of the most heralded books ever written on depression. In that work, Solomon states that to overcome the affliction, we must do more than *just* reconnect with ourselves and others; we must also forget the turmoil that sits right in front of us.[62]

Now, of course, the word· *ignorant* can have several different connotations. When using it here, I'm referring to one of them specifically: the fact that we can choose to be disciplined with our thoughts and overlook some of the things that stress us, even when the rational parts of our brains attempt to convince us otherwise. To make more sense of this idea, let's use climate change and, albeit to a lesser degree, advanced warfare as examples.

Though both subjects often trigger us and demand our attention, giving it to them typically only leads us back to the most formidable kinds of abysses. That's why, instead of contemplating such unsettling ideas, we should try to disregard them altogether and sail in the opposite direction as calmly and quickly as we can; doing so brings us ever closer to our desired goal of intentional ignorance.

And while achieving that goal isn't always a walk in the park, the following two steps can help make it a bit more feasible or straightforward. The first of them is to educate ourselves on what, if anything, we can do to counter or mitigate the concepts or possibilities that demoralize us the most. In the case of climate change, this might mean researching ways to conserve energy and lower our carbon footprint.

The second step is to put our research into action. For example, let's suppose our energy-based investigations suggest we should reduce our consumption of meat and dairy products, move toward a zero-waste lifestyle, and fly less in order to do our part in the fight against global warming. To execute step two, then, we must implement some, if not all, of these recommendations.

Of course, the amount of implementation each of us requires before feeling like we've done enough will vary. That's why, as a rule of thumb, we should simply let our consciences do the talking. For instance, if we cut back on cross-country flights but are still uneasy about our contributions to pollution and planetary overheating, then we likely haven't adequately prevented ourselves from falling into similar, related chasms in the future.

What that means is that our goal here is to keep executing until we're able to say, "I've done pretty much all I can, and I'm ready to focus on other concerns. Though I certainly hope this issue doesn't play out in real life, it won't have come as a direct result of my decisions if it does." That way, the next time our fears on the subject arise, we can remind ourselves that, despite the size and scariness of the matter, continuing to worry about it won't get us any further. This sentiment is the hallmark of intentional ignorance.

Hopefully, after we've carried out these two steps, we'll find that deliberately letting go of whatever it is that's haunting us isn't as challenging a task as it previously appeared. That's not to say it'll be a cinch, however. In truth, frightening and disheartening concepts like global warming, nuclear war, and mass shootings will likely always cause some kind of stir in us. However, once we've taken as much action in regard to them as we feel is necessary, we should be able to mitigate that incitement or, at the very least, allow ourselves to look away from it more readily.

STAYING THE COURSE

Many of us who suffer from anxiety and depression tend to overthink or analyze everything to no end. That being the case, the proposition of intentionally looking away from our greatest fears might seem undesirable or impractical. Heck, we may even look at some of the oblivious people around us, like those polluting Earth's atmosphere with no regard, and think to ourselves, "What complete and total ignoramuses!"

However, being a certain kind of ignorant can positively affect our mental health, and it's what will separate us from the reckless polluters of the world. To explain what I'm getting at with such a statement, I'd like to introduce a framework I refer to as *the four phases of ignorance*. Each phase in this framework helps pinpoint where a specific person is in understanding and dealing with a particular, dreadful subject. What that signifies is, when combined, these four stages form a linear progression through which someone can advance toward proper comprehension and management of such a topic.

First in that progression are those who are unaware of their ignorance. These are the *meta-ignorant, unconsciously ignorant*, or *unintentionally ignorant* folks of the world — the same ones polluting the atmosphere without a care. They don't even realize that what they're doing could potentially be destructive or hurtful.

Though my descriptions of this first phase might make it sound wholly undesirable, there *is* one significant, albeit questionable, benefit to being in it. That benefit is that it saves or rids us of the guilt and pain associated with understanding how our ignorance may be harming others. The problem with that guilt evasion, however, is it's not entirely sustainable. At some point in our lives, something typically comes across our path and informs us of our ignorance. That path crossing activates phase two, where we become *consciously ignorant*.

For the polluters of the world, a phase-shifting event of this nature could take the shape of idling one's car in the driveway for too long and having a neighbor mention that doing so is bad for the environment. Though such a lesson might not always tell these folks exactly why their behavior is destructive, it gives them an opportunity to realize there's something about it they don't yet understand.

Now, of course, not everything a neighbor, friend, or trusted source says to a particular person will get through to him or her. Nor will everyone experience such a *waking-up* moment, despite all the lessons life throws his or her way. However, it's safe to say that, for many people, such a phenomenon does occur at some point. Once it does, these folks will have advanced to this second phase in the process.

The interesting thing about this phase is we rarely spend much time in it. Either we shrug off our neighbors, or we heed their words, open our digital devices, and research what they said to us. Doing the former negates what these folks mentioned and, in time, makes us unconsciously ignorant once more, while doing the latter moves us into phase three, where we become *non-ignorant*.

On a related note, we can also make this quick transition from the first phase to the third in one fell swoop. For example, we might watch a documentary on an important social issue with a friend, despite not knowing anything about the subject. In viewing such a film, we go from being unaware of our ignorance to moderately informed — all in just a couple of hours and with the help of one flick.

Yet, regardless of how we get there, it's in this third phase that we realize what it is we've been oblivious to and come to understand its unsettling nature. Upon entering this troubling point in the progression, we discover two choices: we can either fight endlessly with our new understanding or give ourselves permission to look away from it and move to phase four, where we finally become *intentionally ignorant*.

The first of these options is the simpler one, in the sense that it doesn't require changing our overly analytical ways of thinking. However, it's also the more difficult choice since wrestling with our findings will bring us more downward spirals and states of helplessness in the future. Conversely, while the second option is also challenging to carry out, it's the only one that leads anywhere good.

Luckily, it becomes more manageable once we've taken action to mitigate any destructive outcomes associated with our new learnings, as doing such a thing removes a heavy burden from our consciences. With that burden no longer weighing on us, we can more easily drop our daunting understandings and the cyclical, helpless thinking associated with them. And that, in turn, tends to cause our mental monsters to retreat into the depths of the ocean.

However, every once in a while, they'll poke their heads back up in the form of random conversations, harrowing news headlines, or attention-grabbing push notifications reminding us of our greatest fears. When this inevitably occurs, we must do our best to remember the main takeaway from this chapter: all routes lead to the abyss. Or, I should say, they *can* if we allow them to.

What that means, in more concrete terms, is that even though these reminders are scary, we have to turn away from them and navigate elsewhere, eventually. Otherwise, we'll never get back to everyday life. Such a turning away represents phase four in action — exercising the habit of being intentionally ignorant. And while it may seem counterintuitive, illogical, or irresponsible, it's what we have to do if we want to keep our boats from sinking.

Once we've moved into this fourth phase, we must resolve to stay there for good. One of the reasons that can be so difficult, however, is that our worries sometimes dip underwater for such prolonged periods it seems as if they're gone forever. Sadly, this is but a trick — just because we aren't as concerned about our biggest fears at any given moment doesn't mean they'll never resurface. In all likelihood, they eventually will, and, when they do, they'll test our newfound resolve as best they can.

In reality, when we feel as if they actually *have* withdrawn from our lives, we've more than likely just stopped thinking about them for so long that we've cut off their momentum. However, if we really wanted to rehash our worries, regress to phase three, and send ourselves back into the maelstrom, we could. But that begs the question: why on Earth would we?

Instead of falling prey to such a mistake, we must sail as far and as fast from our aquatic foes as possible, then stay the course as best we can. In practice, this might take the form of unfollowing individuals on social media who regularly rehash the topics that trigger us, avoiding or unsubscribing from sensationalistic publications, or limiting those dreaded, fear-mongering push notifications.

Now, if this all seems a bit radical or over-the-top, that's because it is. But there's a reason for that: the mental health ocean is a treacherous one. If we're not meticulous mariners, we're in for a nightmarish sail across it. As such, we must stick to our charted routes and remember that almost everything we think, see, hear, and read can send us back into the confines of depression if we let it.

DECONSTRUCTING A GYRE

In our society, we tend to say we'll be happy as soon as some particular thing in the distance finally comes into view. For example, when we move out of our parents' house, land our dream job, or save enough money to buy that sleek sports car we've been eyeing.

Though this logic is compelling, it's also a bit hazardous. That's because telling ourselves we can't be happy right now dampens our desire to seek alternative sources of joy, and that, in a deceptive way, is just another form — albeit a mild one — of hopelessness. After all, if we know we need that new Mercedes to be happy, why would we bother looking for jubilation through other means? Of course, I'm being facetious, but I imagine you still see my point.

Another danger with this kind of thinking is it creates high expectations for the future and sets us up for disappointment. That disappointment is a theme that occasionally manifests in our careers, especially for those who've recently, and voluntarily, stopped working. For such folks, discovering that retirement isn't always as joy-producing as expected — at least not without some serious planning — can lead to levels of distress that aren't easy to overcome.[63]

Though I certainly haven't been through such a phenomenon yet myself, I experienced something similar during my 2018 battle with depression — the one I described in the second chapter of this book. Shortly before that battle began, I was working full-time as a salesperson at one of Boston's up-and-coming software development firms. Not very fulfilled in that role, I created a compelling narrative to help me through; I told myself I'd finally be happy when I took back control of my schedule, spent more time writing, and published my first manuscript.

A few months after making that declaration, I landed an accommodating, remote gig as a software engineer. With an offer in hand, I quit my company, began building a mobile app for my first client, and finished what would eventually become the initial entry in the series you're now reading.

Though it was exciting, at first, to make money without even having to show up to an office, that exhilaration quickly faded. Part of the reason for that was that my inaugural assignment only lasted a couple of months; I shipped the app I'd been developing, then moved on to a new, less inspiring project for a different customer.

For that subsequent assignment, my team and I built prototypes to support a large corporation's new product line. While the people on that project were some of the nicest, most professional folks I've ever collaborated with, the work itself was a total bore. And that's when there was any. Most days, so much red tape halted our progress that we just sat at home and twiddled our thumbs.

Despite that lack of progress and my dissatisfaction with it, however, I kept quiet; I didn't want to give up the easy income stream I had going. Sadly, and thanks, in part, to the isolation and boredom associated with that assignment — the kinds so many of us became intimately familiar with during 2020's COVID-19 lockdowns — I quickly fell into the depression I recounted in this book's early pages.

Having already covered that experience in detail, as well as many of its prerequisite, depression-related frameworks, I think we're finally in a place where we can analyze it and extract some helpful insights to apply to future battles. One thing I want to point out about this process, however, is that while we'll discuss some of the common factors behind depression during it, we'll do so in a somewhat generic fashion, understanding that no two experiences with the disease are identical. That way, almost everyone will be able to take something away from the conversation.

So, just what are those generic factors, and what do they typically look like? A lot like the three spheres of our biopsychosocial model not lining up with our expectations of them. Though it's impossible to know how many of those spheres must be off-track for depression to emerge, we *can* say that the higher the number, and with larger degrees to which they are, the greater the likelihood that despair will arise. For example, if we're constantly thinking dark, agonizing thoughts, eating loads of junk food, and working jobs we despise, we're putting ourselves at a very high risk of navigating back to the gyre.

As it applies to my 2018 episode, this same biopsychosocial logic tells us something similar. That is, at the time, all three sections of my model were off-kilter. Though there were several reasons for that, the main ones aren't too difficult to identify in hindsight.

First, since I wasn't walking to work anymore, I wasn't using physical activity to clear my head as much as I had in the past. Second, because I was so isolated, I wasn't connecting with very many people. And third, because I was so secluded, sedentary, and uninspired, I was continually jumping into my head and rehashing some of the worst thoughts imaginable.

And, to top it all off, I was still reeling from a disappointment I didn't want to admit to myself — the fact that I'd gotten to the "when" of my "I'll be happy" narrative, and, somehow, was still nowhere near joyous. As the saying goes, "Man plans, and God laughs."[64]

Sadly, I didn't know what to do during that bout other than consume content on mental health. Though it wasn't the worst strategy of all time, looking back on it, I wish I'd been more courageous and open with others about my experiences. That likely would've helped me discover some valuable resources and move toward recovery more quickly.

However, since content consumption was the path I chose, I set out to finish as many self-help and depression-related books as I could get my hands on. Thankfully, several of them contained wisdom that allowed me to make more sense of my struggles and pushed me to carry out some much-needed changes in my life.

The first of those books was psychologist Barry Schwartz's best-selling title, *The Paradox of Choice*. In it, Schwartz showed me that learned helplessness, at face value, doesn't tell the whole story when it comes to depression. Instead, it's the context of that helplessness that matters most. Specifically, when it results from some temporary circumstance, we rarely fall into prolonged despair. However, when it stems from a global, chronic, or personal issue, we usually do.[65]

Yet, the funny thing about these categorizations is we can often influence them to a degree. That is, we can choose to see many of our challenges in life as more temporary or impersonal than meets the eye. For example, in my situation, though my struggles with global warming and my grandmother's passing clearly fit into more lasting categories, my work-related disappointment did not. I'd just temporarily convinced myself it did.

As I looked deeper, I saw that my disillusionment with my "I'll be happy when" statement and work-from-home jobs, in general, was telling me I'd never find a role I truly enjoyed. When I bought into that idea, I couldn't help but feel dejected. However, when I reframed that disappointment by telling myself there was indeed something out there for me, and I'd just have to keep looking for it, I loosened my hopelessness' grip on me.

Another enlightening thing I gleaned from that book had to do with perception, state management, and the father of Cognitive Therapy, Aaron Beck. At the time, though I'd been familiar with Beck's Cognitive Triad for a couple of years, I'd never seen a reason to use it. After all, I hadn't been depressed since well before learning of it.

However, that changed when I read Schwartz's *Paradox of Choice*. As I digested his points on learned helplessness, a lightbulb went off in my mind, highlighting the link between them, Beck, and the second jib from our "Triangular Sails" discussion. Given my previous lack of use of that jib, I'm confident I wouldn't have seen that connection if not for the despair-filled state in which I'd been.

Shortly after that lightbulb moment, I realized that if I wanted to end my depression, I'd have to stop viewing the world and the future so dismally. And, just as importantly, I'd have to stop telling myself it wasn't okay to struggle despite achieving the work-life setup for which I'd long yearned.

The second book that helped me persevere through my difficulties was *The 50th Law* by Robert Greene and 50 Cent. In that book, Greene reminded me that, when thrust into freedom, our minds tend to gravitate toward unnerving possibilities of all shapes and sizes.[66] Though I'd learned that lesson previously, just like Beck's Cognitive Triad, I hadn't yet applied it to my situation — mainly because I was so preoccupied with and blinded by my despair.

However, when I stopped to think about it, I realized how relevant it was to my situation as well as many of my previous writings. For instance, as we covered in the first book in this series, our brains are survival machines.[67] They're constantly on the lookout for potential threats to our well-being. As soon as they find one, they sound the alarms.

While this is an undoubtedly great feature as it pertains to our subsistence, it comes at a price. That price is the fact that, even after we've neutralized all immediate threats, our anxious minds keep working, guarding, analyzing, and obsessing. What that means is, without something to distract them from their vigilance in these situations, they typically turn to larger, more looming concerns, such as existence or death.

This preoccupation with vast, unsettling ideas is the same thing I experienced during my own battle, and it's what revisits me from time to time when I let my guard down and fail to fill my schedule with engaging activities. It's also a primary reason folks struggle when they retire. Without the intellectual or physical stimulation of work, their psyches often drift into darkness and focus on some of life's scariest subjects.

To avoid such subjects and the existential angst that comes with them, we must leverage the social part of our biopsychosocial model by giving ourselves fun or challenging tasks to perform and deep connections on which to lean. Those tasks and connections can be anything we choose, such as sinking our teeth into new hobbies, volunteering for causes we care about, or spending time with our families. Whatever helps keep our eyes off the abyss.

Related to the illuminating points Greene makes in *The 50th Law* were two other fascinating ones I read from authors Jordan Peterson and William Styron. In his colossal book, *Maps of Meaning*, Peterson states that when we're engaging in work we find meaningful, death is often the last thing on our minds. However, when we're toiling through jobs we don't enjoy, our demise tends to feel like it's right around the corner.[68]

That might also be why Styron, in his short, depression-focused memoir, *Darkness Visible*, says the feeling that life is slipping away at an accelerated pace is a trademark of the disease.[69] Sometimes, it's almost as if our bodies know we're not living the way we want to and send us into despair to make us address that discrepancy. Sure, I could just be jumping to conclusions in saying such a thing, but I know that when my own life felt like it was slipping away, I definitely wasn't living in an inspired fashion or doing the kind of work Peterson recommends.

THE WORMHOLE TO THE ABYSS

One final author whose back catalog I browsed during this same period was Leo Tolstoy. Though I only scratched the surface with his writing, I found what I did read to be moving and deeply philosophical. I'm not alone in saying that, either. Many refer to him as one of the greatest authors of all time.

In one of his more famous pieces, a short, dark autobiography entitled *A Confession*, Tolstoy recounts an existential crisis he suffered and the struggles that came with it. Reading that work floored me; so much of what I'd faced during my European getaway, and the months that followed, overlapped with what he recalled in it. Specifically, much as I'd done, he wrestled with one of the most profound questions of all: "If death is inevitable, then what's the meaning or point of life?"[70]

The most interesting thing about that question, at least to me, was that Tolstoy never really came up with an answer. What he did conclude, however, was that no matter how much he fought with it or told himself he needed a solution before he could start living again, he never would be able to resolve it. So, instead of continuing to ask it, he held on through his struggles in hopes of one day reconnecting with life, finding God in everyday experiences, and infusing meaning into those experiences through that reconnection.

Finishing that book led me to four of the most critical conclusions I made during my entire crisis. The first of them was that if we're asking ourselves the deepest, darkest questions about life, then we're absolutely in our heads, and we're in big trouble until we cease doing so. After all, not even Leo Tolstoy could find answers to those questions, so I don't think we'll be able to, either. Rather than repeatedly torment ourselves, we should stop asking them altogether.

The second conclusion I made stems back to something we touched upon earlier in this book — the concept that, sometimes, "the problem is not the problem." As it pertains to our current discussion, this statement suggests that it's not our lack of answers to such deep, philosophical questions that drives our depression. Instead, it's the fact that we've fallen into a destructive state and disconnected from life itself. Sometimes, like Tolstoy, we need to reconnect and regain our passion for everyday experiences. Then, hopefully, our insistence on answering such queries will disappear.

The third conclusion was that, because Tolstoy's question is arguably the deepest one out there, if we answer it pessimistically, we subject ourselves to the mother of all abysses. As obvious as it may sound, since none of us want to experience that force, we should refrain from such negativity as best we can.

The fourth and final conclusion was that all abysses have wormholes — hidden, immediate paths back to them that open as we sail away from them. What that means is, we can transport ourselves back into any mental whirlpool in an instant without even realizing it. All it takes is one simple, despair-related question.

To illustrate and flesh out this concept, let's revisit our discussion on unhappy retirees and assume that we, too, are dissatisfied after exiting the workforce. Now, if we wanted to enter the abyss over our retirement-related disillusionment normally, all we'd have to do is think about how much time we spent in pursuit of a goal that didn't end up being as gratifying as we thought it would. But, of course, we know better than that, so we won't — crisis averted, right? Not so fast. It's at *this* moment the wormhole opens.

To enter that hole, all we have to do is ask a more pessimistic, Tolstoy-like question about the subject at hand. This drops us right back into the vortex without us initially knowing we're in it. For example, instead of dwelling on the fact that our retirement isn't as exciting as we thought it would be, we can teleport back to the chasm simply by asking, "If I waited this long to stop working and it isn't what I expected, then is anything in life ever as good as anticipated?" As you can imagine, this is not only a perilous question to put forth — it's also a sign that we're, unsuspectingly, in our heads once more.

And while it may sound crazy or like none of us would ever make such inquiries, we do all the time. We just don't always realize it because we don't see these questions as crazy when we pose them — we see them as rational. To avoid or seal up our wormholes, we have to drop such daunting and all-encompassing questions as soon as they arise. Otherwise, a surprise wave or wind could very well shoot us back into the maw of the maelstrom.

SAILING INTO SUFFERING

Throughout this book, I've used many words to describe depression and its accompanying symptoms and feelings. While some of those words have been literal representations of the affliction, like helplessness and hopelessness, others have been symbolic, such as abyss, gyre, and vortex. Regardless of which kind I put forth, however, my underlying message is the same, and it's one that reveals an unsettling fact of existence.

That fact is that depression is a type of suffering, and, in life, we can't escape all forms of distress entirely. Or, as Nietzsche once said, "to live is to suffer." Now, that's not to say life is and *only* is suffering, nor that we can't evade specific kinds of it altogether — just that some amount of one of its many varieties, depression included, is inevitable.

When we think about this quote critically, we see that even those who live most comfortably eventually have to face its truth. In time, life confronts us all with the difficulties of change, loss, failure, and our unavoidable mortalities. In other words, there's simply no way to circumvent all forms of hardship forever. But, the good news is, we likely wouldn't want to, even if we could, as such a fate comes with its own price tag, and, spoiler alert, it's none other than more suffering.

NOT ALL SUFFERING IS CREATED EQUAL

SAILING INTO SUFFERING

When I say everyone suffers, I mean that in both the short and the long term. Being human, we all endure disappointment, misfortune, and tragedy from time to time — albeit to widely varying degrees. Yet, though we don't all experience significant forms of distress every day, we do greet smaller doses of it regularly. We call these more manageable instances *discomforts*. And while facing them is a form of suffering in and of itself, it's a more beneficial one than likely meets the eye. Here's why.

By definition, the word discomfort refers to any slight pain we may experience; when we analyze our daily routines, we see they're chock-full of it. That's because achieving our goals — such as getting ahead in our careers, raising happy children, or staying healthy — requires lots of hard work and discipline. While that work is undoubtedly unpleasant at times, we engage in it anyway because of the payoffs we think it will eventually provide us — hence its beneficial nature.

Of course, without the excitement of those rewards fueling us, we'd be much less likely to push through that unpleasantness. But that doesn't change the fact that, as much as we want to bring such payoffs to fruition, it still hurts to wake up at the crack of dawn and sit in traffic, change a diaper, or slog through a group fitness class — and that's why we don't always follow through with the tasks required for accomplishing our desired aims.

Another reason we sometimes eschew our daily dose of discomfort is that, subconsciously, we assume saying *no* to it means being done with it for good, or at least for a good, long while. But that's not how discomfort works. Instead, it hovers around us all the time, even when we engage with it or push it away temporarily.

Now, I know that sounds daunting, but let me assure you, it's a favorable thing overall. That's because there are both positive and negative kinds of suffering, and when we continually embrace the former, we help keep the latter at bay. To make better sense of what I'm talking about here, we'll look at the following fictitious example.

Let's say you hold a prestigious, though stressful, finance job in the city. Every morning, before heading to the office, you wake up early, take your dog for a three-mile run, and throw together a healthy lunch to bring to work. Some days, however, you find it quite challenging to get out of bed.

On these particular mornings, you say to yourself, "If I could just get an extra hour of sleep each day and stop eating those crappy lunches, I'd be so much happier." In turn, you decide to put your morning runs with Fido on hold and ditch your daily meal prep sessions in favor of trips to the sandwich joints near your office.

Six months after that decision, you wake up and realize your life has changed a bit. Not only are you now out of shape, but you also haven't saved anywhere near the amount you said you would. As a result, you have no choice but to re-up your lease with your messy roommate, even though you swore you'd be getting your own place this year.

To make matters worse, you've adjusted to your new, extended sleep schedule and now find it just as hard to get out of bed as you did before you canned your early workouts with your pooch. And, last but not least, at your doctor's appointment yesterday, your physician told you your blood pressure was way up over last year's reading. If you don't get your act together — and soon — you'll run the risk of developing some pretty undesirable ailments.

You're not exactly sure how things could've come to this. You assumed you would've been happier and less stressed if you just lived a more comfortable lifestyle. Yet, you attained that comfort, and you still don't feel either of those things. Instead, all you've achieved as a result of your dates with the snooze button, and many greasy, grilled cheese sandwiches, are a withered bank account, elevated blood pressure, and a decent dose of misery.

So, just how did this happen? In reality, you traded many smaller forms of discomfort, such as waking up early and eating right, for a larger dose of suffering — the despair associated with having saved less money and fallen out of shape. This takeaway leads to one simple, critical fact, and it's that you can, and often do, find some kind of pain in every aspect of your life, no matter your approach. Now, before we get too grim here, we need to make two related, uplifting distinctions.

The first is that not all varieties of suffering are created equal; some are massive, prolonged hurts, while others are smaller, possibly even beneficial, annoyances. The second is, to ward off many of the larger ones, we must purposefully expose ourselves to

116

the smaller ones, especially when we realize the good they could bring us, such as higher savings account balances or slimmer waistlines. When we instead avoid such advantageous discomforts, they stack on top of one another until they cause us immense pain or bring us face-to-face with our dreaded sea monsters.

If you've ever watched a family member retire before, you may have seen this harmful stacking in action. Though retirement promises total paradise and freedom, such things aren't always as they seem, for with that freedom comes time. And lots of it. If we don't fill that time with structure, discipline, and excitement, it's often not long before our chaotic minds take over, and we spend most of our waking hours fixating on problems and fears.

As confusing and painful as this reality may be, however, there's a helpful truth behind it. That truth is that while many of us dream of a day when we can do absolutely nothing, most of us don't quite want that, per se. Instead, what we really desire is the flexibility to live life on our terms — to pack our calendars with fun, engaging, and meaningful events. And while our school or work routines don't always provide such flexibility, they expose us to the discomforts required for keeping our focus off the abyss, growing, and achieving. To put it another way, though they're not perfect, they can be vital to our mental health.

ANTIFRAGILITY AND VOLUNTARY DISCOMFORT

SAILING INTO SUFFERING

In his impactful book, *Antifragile*, economist Nassim Nicholas Talib explains how some things in life break or wear down when exposed to stress and disorder. Such things are what we describe as *fragile*. However, some objects and organisms not only thrive in the presence of such conditions — they also deteriorate in their absence. These items and creatures are what we define as *antifragile*.[71]

As Talib states, humans belong to this second category. That is, we need risk and challenge to survive, just as a glass bowl needs to avoid hitting the pavement. Put differently, when we fail to exercise, we fall out of shape, and when we stop learning new things on the job, our skills and output decrease, and we risk losing our positions. This logic is the same kind that guided our discussion a moment ago.

When we think about the organizations and institutions to which we belong, we see they foster this antifragile nature of ours, especially at a young age. Starting in kindergarten and lasting throughout college, report cards, athletic competitions, and dance recitals force us to stay on our toes, both literally and figuratively, as we strive to hone our skills and keep pace with our peers. Lucky for us, one of the best things about these activities and challenges is, to reap their growth-promoting benefits, all we have to do is show up to class and take our pick of them.

Yet, as we get older and graduate into the real world, these same advantageous opportunities become less readily available. As a result, we have to actively seek out competitions, public performances, and uplifting trials on our own. Unfortunately for us, however, we don't always do such a thing.

In other words, though we sometimes joined sports leagues in our youth simply because all our classmates already had, and we didn't want to be the odd ones out, in the real world, we rarely receive that same sort of pressure. As such, we often go years without participating in activities that test and empower us. In such situations, it's not until disappointment or discontentment comes along and shakes us that we realize we're stuck and need to push ourselves into the same kinds of favorable stress our earlier years provided. It's at that precise moment we recognize the importance of *voluntary discomfort*.

Though I hinted at this concept throughout the previous section, it's now time to call it by name. This practice, made popular by a group of philosophers known as the Stoics, is one in which we expose ourselves to mild forms of difficulty and austerity, so we don't begin to take our good fortunes for granted. As it pertains to everyday experiences, voluntary discomfort is like our nagging childhood babysitter — the one who constantly reminded us to turn off our video games and go run around outside. It teaches us that while sitting on the couch all weekend likely sounds better than exercising, doing so isn't ideal for our long-term physical and mental health.

To implement this practice ourselves, instead of avoiding manageable difficulties and letting our days melt together, we must embrace such challenges, as doing so sets us up to enjoy their eventual conclusions and better appreciate our contemporary blessings. As crazy as it may sound, a more extreme example of this sort of thing would be to sleep on the floor once in a while, so we don't forget how comfortable our mattresses are. After all, one night's rest on the cold, hard ground is usually all we need to regain our appreciation for our beds.

At the root of this kind of reasoning are two fundamental principles. The first is the notion that everything in life is relative or that how we evaluate our lives and the things in them is a product of the comparisons we make.

For example, when we juxtapose our possessions with those of the wealthiest people we know, we often lose our excitement for them. Yet when we instead think about what life was like just one or two hundred years ago, we realize we now have it better, in many ways, than kings and queens of centuries past — minus the servants, of course. We have access to new, breakthrough treatments and medical procedures, travel long distances for relatively cheap, and manage our schedules on cell phones 100,000 times more powerful than the computer behind the first moon landing.[72]

What makes voluntary discomfort such a powerful tool, then, is that it forces us to reconnect to these sorts of uplifting comparisons much more frequently. By temporarily taking away some of our present-day luxuries, it pushes us into gratitude mode and more empowering evaluations of our circumstances. These refreshed perspectives boost our mood and drive us to seek out additional tolerable challenges in the future.

The second core principle underlying voluntary discomfort is the idea that our environments influence how we act through a complex system of rewards and punishments. In psychology, there's a term for the process by which such a thing occurs — *operant conditioning* — and it's at play in all our home, work, and school lives.[73]

When we study hard or log extra hours to help meet a client's deadline, our professors and bosses bestow good grades, praises, or even bonuses upon us. In the world of operant conditioning, these rewards are known as *positive reinforcers*. They tell us we did something good and that if we do similar things in the future, we'll likely get recompensed comparably.

The same general logic, when reversed, applies to undesirable behaviors as well. When we fail to carry out our teachers' and boss' demands, they give us poor marks or scold us. These punishments push us to try harder or follow directions more closely next time.

Now, if you're hoping to get ahead of me here by thinking, "These penalties must be what *negative reinforcers* are," good try — but not so fast. In reality, this second kind of reinforcer describes something different altogether, and, no, it's not punitive. Instead, it's the unpleasant stimuli we avoid or eliminate after performing a specific action, such as the burns we evade by applying sunblock or the annoying sounds we suppress in our cars by finally buckling our seatbelts.

Though both types of reinforcement regularly influence our behavior across all sorts of scenarios and situations, many of us are more familiar with the positive kind after spending years chasing all the different carrots dangling in front of us. And while there's nothing inherently wrong with such a pursuit, it does have one flaw — it tempts us to set our sights on the next carrot and discount or overlook the ones we've already accumulated. That problem is one that practitioners of voluntary discomfort don't run into nearly as often as the rest of us.

Since these folks purposefully inject austerity into their lives, they're better able to appreciate the carrots they've collected over the years. When they spend a month walking to the grocery store instead of driving, they remember just how much they need and love their vehicles. Rather than constantly searching for their next high-end sports car, these ambitious souls utilize negative reinforcement by seeking out, pushing through, and later removing the good-kinds-of-pain, all in the name of generating gratitude for what they already have.

In reality, we need both forms of reinforcement to maintain a healthy perspective in life. However, one of the problems with our society's invisible conditioning system is that it favors the positive kind and distracts us from the benefits of voluntary discomfort. By default, and in the long run, this spoils us and leads us to take what we have for granted. Though we've covered that idea of becoming spoiled a bit already, I have one more example of it that I think you'll find amusing. This one comes from an old, popular TV series.

In the twenty-eighth episode of *The Twilight Zone*, we watch as a man named Rocky is shot while attempting to flee the scene of a pawnshop heist. After briefly getting knocked out by the gunfire, Rocky wakes up and realizes he's miraculously unharmed. Confused, he turns and sees a man named Pip, who says he'll take Rocky around town and give him anything he wants.

After countless unexplainable occurrences, Rocky surmises he must've died during the robbery and, as a result, is now in heaven. After all, why else would Pip have just given him a gourmet meal, a beautiful woman to socialize with, and one million dollars? Content with his conclusion, Rocky blissfully dances with his new female companion, then heads to the casino. There, he's not surprised to find that he wins every bet he makes.

About one month later, Rocky grows bored of his winning ways and invites Pip to his apartment. Upon his guardian's arrival, Rocky says he's fed up with the predetermined nature of his new setting and wants something fun and challenging for a change. In response, Pip recommends that Rocky do what he did on earth — rob a bank. After stepping through the details, however, Rocky dismisses the idea, stating that even a bank heist would be preordained in his new environment, and that would be no fun either.

At his wit's end, Rocky tells Pip he wants out of heaven and that he'll go nuts if he doesn't get his way. Desperate, he pleads to take a trip to "the other place" — hell. Realizing Rocky still doesn't know the nature of his new surroundings, Pip replies, "Heaven? Whatever gave you the idea you were in heaven? This *is* the other place!" Terrified, Rocky rushes to open his apartment door and run away, only to realize he's trapped inside. The credits then roll as Pip laughs at his prisoner's anguish.

Though there are many ways to interpret this spooky story, we must avoid the readily accessible yet pessimistic ones. Otherwise, we may get ourselves in some serious mental trouble. One easy thing to do would be to react with negativity or ask dark questions that shoot us back through the wormhole to the abyss. For example, we could look at Rocky's situation and say to ourselves, "Wait a minute. If getting everything I've ever wanted still won't make me happy, then what's the point of even striving for it?"

As we talked about in the last chapter, these sorts of questions are just fancy ways of getting back in our heads. In reality, happiness, much like depression, is a complex subject. But just because that's the case, that doesn't mean we need to go and throw ourselves a full-blown pity party. There *are* some uplifting, albeit counterintuitive, explanations on happiness, and we'll get to them. I promise. But, first, we need to hold off the oncoming mental storm.

If we look past the pessimism, however, I think we're able to see some of the more useful takeaways associated with Rocky's plight. After all, I don't recite his tale to scare you but to reinforce two similar, essential lessons on the dangers of not leaning into discomfort. The first is that avoiding uncomfortable feelings, tasks, and situations only leads to more suffering in the long run. The second is that, without gratitude and growth-promoting kinds of pain in our lives, our blessings and good fortunes eventually spoil us.

As we saw in the *Twilight Zone* story, despite evading all forms of uncertainty and hardship, Rocky was bored and restless. By the end of the episode, he was practically begging to lose a bet or give away his winnings. This sort of thing epitomizes the first of our two discomfort-related lessons. Now, of course, it's not like Rocky was purposefully avoiding challenges — he just wasn't allowed to engage in them. But, for our purposes, we can pretend as though that was the case. Either way, no suffering simply means *more* suffering.

As we also witnessed along Rocky's journey, despite getting everything he ever dreamed of, he quickly became disillusioned and sick of it. This is what it looks like when the second of our discomfort-based lessons comes to life. Though Rocky's boredom may *seem* crazy, it's not all that surprising. After all, without being mindful of and grateful for what we have, our psyches and bodies can adapt to our circumstances and grow tired of them. This is especially true when we don't have negative stimuli with which to compare our current situations and remind ourselves of the good things in our lives.

In reality, Rocky felt so uneasy in his new environment because, just like us, he's antifragile; his inability to encounter uncertainty or advantageous stress drove him crazy. And while I'm sure we'd all be quick to claim that we'd never get sick of having all our own dreams magically and perpetually come true, the information we covered in this chapter would seem to suggest the opposite.

As such, we'd be wise to take Rocky's lessons to heart. If we embraced our antifragile ways, challenged ourselves regularly, and continually leaned into discomfort, we'd give ourselves a better chance of evading the abyss in the long term. And since we eventually get accustomed, even addicted, to almost everything we do, why not let those very things be the counterintuitive, empowering ones we outlined here?

COMMITTING TO DISCOMFORT

As you've probably experienced in your own life, we humans aren't always great at pushing ourselves into pain and delaying gratification for more significant payoffs down the road. We often take those extra slices of pizza, hit the snooze button too many times, and skip meaningful conversations with friends, not realizing what all those seemingly harmless actions might add up to one day.

Yet, even when we do recognize that embracing challenges might help us manage our depression, we're still sometimes missing an essential prerequisite for carrying out such a plan. That requirement is knowing that the juice of our efforts will be worth the proverbial squeeze. Without such an understanding, we'll see difficulty on the horizon and decide we'd much rather sail elsewhere. Or, worse: we'll choose not to sail at all.

Oddly enough, this insight brings us back to the Nietzsche quote with which I more or less opened this chapter. As we now revisit it, I must make a confession. When I initially referenced it, I intentionally withheld its second half. Though I'll admit that move was a bit misleading, such an omission was not without careful consideration; I wanted to layer its message with the content we just finished discussing and save its more uplifting, latter part for this final, unifying section.

So, while he did say, "to live is to suffer," he also said, right afterward, "to survive is to find meaning in the suffering." And that's the final message of this chapter: To carry on in both life and depression, we must find something that gives purpose to our inevitable pain. We must discover and embrace our juice-producing pursuits. If we don't, we risk exposing ourselves to utter despair.

Though there are countless categories and flavors of these sorts of things, the most common ones include the missions, causes, and people we care about most. Once we've chosen one or several of them, we can hold them close as we take on challenges in our daily lives. They're our inspiration for continuing forward, and they provide us with meaning and purpose during even the most trying of times.

As an example, we might push through difficult fitness classes because we want to be healthy, vibrant, and present for our families. Or, we might work long hours at our municipal jobs, despite our bosses breathing down our necks, because we know the work we're doing is helping the less fortunate members of our communities.

If we don't find such meaning in our daily struggles, we'll quickly reach a point where we feel the effort we exert is not worth the payoff we receive. Of course, that's not to say everything we do has to benefit us directly. It's just that if our struggles aren't helping *someone*, it won't be long before we ask ourselves, "What's the point?" And, with that question come our old, gyrating friends: helplessness and hopelessness.

Thus, what we have to do is figure out what kind of suffering we're willing to tolerate and how we'll derive our own forms of meaning as we endure it. For me, depression is one of the varieties for which I have little patience. Though it's usually quite challenging to push through, when I'm depressed, I remind myself that sitting on the couch and rehashing my troubles will do me no good.

These reminders serve to propel me into positive forms of discomfort, such as exercising, writing, or podcasting. You know, the ones that will not only distract me from my aquatic demons but also possibly help others and, in turn, reconnect me with my own purpose and reasons for persisting.

And while we're all going to suffer on some level, no matter what we do in life, how we suffer — and to what degree — is often up to us. If we choose the forms of discomfort that inspire us, help us grow, and allow us to give back, we'll keep some of the larger, more agonizing ones underwater. And, more importantly, we'll develop the character and confidence to valiantly battle our sea monsters when they do emerge from the depths of the ocean.

AT RISK OF CAPSIZING

As we discussed in the chapter entitled "Triangular Sails," the concept of stabilizing and balancing our boats is essential when it comes to our mental health. If we don't leverage the jibs of our vessels properly, wind and waves can rush in and tip us to one side or the other. Once those forces move us far enough in either direction, it becomes challenging to recenter ourselves.

Worse yet, the more off-balance we get, the closer we come to capsizing altogether. Not only is this a sailor's worst nightmare, but it's also the easiest way to get swept into an abyss. After all, how can we possibly steer ourselves away from one if we aren't right-side up?

When it comes to depression, losing balance can take many different forms. One example of this unsteadiness is having *any* of the three sections of our biopsychosocial model get thrown off course. Such a thing regularly transpires when we endure personal tragedies or suffer grave misfortunes.

Namely, when we lose someone we love, our loss often creates such a radical shift in our social world that we fall out of balance and into despair, regardless of any other changes occurring in our lives. What can deter us from going to that dark place, however, is the degree to which the remaining aspects of our model support us.

For example, sometimes, our friends and family members pick us up, keep us busy, and help us grieve in a manageable fashion. Such actions allow us to put more distance between our boats and the abyss. Given enough of that space — as well as time and care — it's possible we avoid those dreaded maelstroms altogether.

Occasionally, however, our tribulations instead pull our biological and psychological spheres out of whack with them. In the case of losing someone, that means we're dealt several brutal blows at once — the pain of the tragedy itself, the fact that our sorrow tends to keep us housebound or bedridden, and the extra time our confinement gives us to ruminate. During this time, we may ask ourselves some of life's most unsolvable questions, such as, "Where did my loved one go?" or, "Will I ever see this person again?" These questions serve as immediate entry points into our heads as well as the abyss itself.

While losing someone is undeniably difficult to go through, it's not the only way we can fall out of balance in the mental health realm. For instance, sometimes, we instead float into depression via a sort of death-by-a-thousand-paper-cuts experience. In such scenarios, there's no massive misfortune or tragedy that sinks us. Instead, several challenging events and stimuli stack on top of one another and gradually push us underwater.

This sort of imbalance looks a lot like the kind we saw in the chapter entitled "Scylla, Meet Charybdis" and the experiment involving mice and the UCMS protocol. Over an extended period, countless persistent stressors and hurts slowly take the wind out of our sails until, one day, we wake up and realize we're both off-balance and motionless.

THE BLESSING AND THE CURSE OF CONSCIOUSNESS

While there are innumerable ways by which we could meet our capsized fate, the most common one tends to start in our heads. Why's that? Because, unlike grief-promoting forces in our biological and social spheres — such as injuring ourselves or losing our jobs — negative thoughts are always at our disposal. And, to send ourselves back to the chasm, all we have to do is contemplate any one of them.

Yet, even though our minds are a primary source of our distress, it's obviously not practical or feasible to turn them off indefinitely or do away with them. And while we certainly need to quiet them from time to time — such as during get-togethers or athletic competitions — we wouldn't be the wonderful, conscious beings we are today if we no longer had them.

This paradox leads me to an admittedly strange conclusion, and it's that consciousness is both a blessing and a curse. Despite the peculiarity of that idea, however, I felt it necessary to discuss given its overlap with our equilibrium-based conversation. Now, if that connection isn't apparent just yet, not to worry. The following example should help bring it to light a bit more.

AT RISK OF CAPSIZING

If you've ever gone to the dog park or been around people who own canines, you'll know how much most humans love them. When we see these happy animals, we sometimes say things to ourselves like, "What I wouldn't give to be that joyous pup right now! He doesn't have a care or worry in the world!" And while I'm sure we make such declarations facetiously, there's a hint of truth lurking below the surface here.

That truth is that, to some degree, it would be freeing to regress to a level of consciousness akin to that of our furry pals — one that doesn't lead to despair nearly as often as our own. It would be liberating, in many ways, not to get stuck obsessing over fears of the future. And it would be a huge relief to know we never again have to experience the pain associated with thinking about sad or scary possibilities on the horizon.

For, as far as we know, though animals can certainly experience negative emotions, they don't spend nearly as much time in their heads as we do. Instead, they focus on the here and now, going about their cheerful business minute by minute until one day, before they realize it, they're gone.

And while it's tempting to believe that such a carefree fate might be one we'd love to attain, I think we'd be missing the point if we genuinely bought into such an idea. That's because when we consider the alluring possibility of being freed from the dark recesses of our minds, we forget it's those same recesses that allow us to live the beautiful lives we do. To plan, create art, seek happiness, have deep conversations, love one another, and be fully human. Those upsides, and that downside — at least at the moment — can't be separated.

So, how do we resolve this discrepancy? Well, I hate to break it to you, but since we probably won't become super-dogs overnight, we may just need to embrace what we have. Of course, I write that with a smile on my face. In reality, I'd say that, despite our episodic existential struggles, we've got a pretty good thing going with this whole humanity idea.

However, one thing we *can* do is learn from our four-legged friends. We can realize we sometimes fall out of equilibrium in our psychological worlds and get too far in our heads. We can understand how that misalignment not only brings about despair but also sometimes reinforces the same cerebral, chemical imbalances that led to our depression in the first place. Seeing our carefree pets reminds us of these notions and tells us to live more in our hearts and the present moment.

When we do that, we unlock the full potential of our consciousness — the ability to be here, right now, and reap the rewards of thoughtfully planning for the future. And though it may occasionally feel as if our minds are our worst enemies, we must remember such feelings are more a product of our states than they are reality. When we get out of our heads, whether through spending time with loved ones or listening to our favorite songs, we see the benefits of these fickle structures more clearly.

DRAWING UPON ANCIENT WISDOM

No school of thought centers itself around the concept of balance more strongly than that of Daoism. Via this ancient Chinese philosophy, we learn it's the offsetting of seemingly opposing forces that allows for a vast number of natural phenomena to occur.[74] Though this principle is prevalent throughout Daoism's various teachings, in few places is it more apparent than the philosophy's primary symbol — the yin-yang.[75]

On that symbol, we see a circle containing a pair of similar, interlocking, teardrop-like shapes — a black one with a white dot on the right and a white one with a black dot on the left. These two figures represent the yin and the yang, respectively.

In the abstract, the former refers to feminine, universal energies, while the latter pertains to masculine ones. In the real world, yin and yang take on a whole host of paradoxical complements, such as war and peace, heart and head living, or chaos and order. What these rivaling powers do *not* represent, however, is the battle of good versus evil, as both of them are necessary and beneficial. That is, assuming they stay in harmony with one another.

At the end of the first book in this series, I told a story that highlighted the significance of thinking and living in a fashion that balances these two forces. While on a Hawaiian getaway in early 2018, my family and I received notifications on our cell phones saying a ballistic missile was heading for the island. Fearing the worst, we huddled in the common room and waited for the end to come. Luckily and surprisingly, however, those notifications turned out to be false alarms; just a few days later, we returned home safely.

Though we were all grateful to make it out of that situation unscathed, the experience still shook some of us. Especially me. One of the main things it made me see was I'd gotten comfortable treading water in life and disconnected from the finitude of my time on Earth. As a result, I'd drifted off course with some of my biggest goals and dreams, assuming I'd get to them later. Realizing the path I was on was one that would likely end in regret, I chose to view the situation as a wake-up call, a much-needed reminder to get back to pursuing what I deemed most important.

In the months following that life-changing experience, however, I fell out of balance in a different fashion by taking this new perspective a bit too seriously. I reminded myself of my mortality so often it debilitated me and robbed me of my energy and excitement. Now, that's not to say I concluded it's a *bad* strategy, just that its effectiveness comes down to the exact ways by which we use it. In my case, I'd gone from not utilizing it whatsoever — all yin — to leveraging it to the point of madness — all yang.

When I made that drastic and unproductive jump, I learned a vital yet painful lesson: While it's okay to reconnect to our mortalities to motivate ourselves, as with all strategies, we need balance. When we forget our time on Earth is limited, we tend to grow complacent about what we want to accomplish in life. However, when we constantly focus on that concept, we freak ourselves out and increase our risk of experiencing a Tolstoy-like crisis — one in which the magnitude of the idea of death saps our enthusiasm for all the fun that's yet to unfold in our lives.

In a book I referenced earlier, *Maps of Meaning*, author Jordan Peterson puts forth a similar argument. Specifically, he mentions how Daoism teaches us that pathology emerges from an excess of yin or yang — an imbalance between the two.[76] Thus, if becoming unbalanced in life is one of the main things that cause our despair to proliferate, it seems only fitting we put into place some process that serves as a line of defense against such a fate.

Given the abstract nature of the notions of yin and yang, there are countless such methodologies we could discuss and adopt. That's why, instead of getting lost in all those different ideas, I'd like to put forth one high-level concept that I think helps us strike a balance between abandoning our desires in life altogether and obsessing over them to the point of burnout.

That concept is the simple practice of creating and maintaining what I call a *life-helm diagram*. These diagrams serve as visual representations of our satisfaction with the most important areas of our lives. They also indicate how well-suited we are to navigate nearby obstacles, storms, and abysses on our oceanic journeys.

As with most ships' steering wheels, these drawings feature spokes and handles sticking out from a central hub, visually dividing them into sectors. On real-life helms, these sections are uniform in width. However, for our diagrams, we'll make them as wide or narrow as we desire, depending on how much we value each of the life categories they represent.

For example, we could dedicate two-thirds of our wheels to the domains of family, physical health, relationships, and spirituality and save the final third for the areas of adventure, career, and finances — assuming that accurately reflects what's valuable to us. Or, we could add or subtract a few ideas from that list and assign individual widths to each one. The options here are limitless — the only requirements are that we choose the categories most meaningful to us, ensure their respective sizes come together to form a complete circle, and draw that preliminary figure on paper.

After completing those three tasks, we should give ourselves a satisfaction score, out of ten, in regard to each domain. Once we've done so, we can redraw our metaphorical steering wheels. The higher the score for a specific section, the taller that part of the diagram will be. And though that doesn't quite fit the design of a real helm, I hope the analogy here makes this concept a bit easier to understand.

Once we've sketched our score-based diagrams, we should step back and look at them as if they were actual steering wheels on a ship. As with real boats, the smaller the helm, the more revolutions required to get our vessels moving in new directions. For us, this means that if the radii of our drawings are short, we'll have to work harder to overcome obstacles and make progress in our lives.

And while it's certainly appealing to have a larger wheel, the most critical aspect of our helms is actually the "evenness" of them. To understand why that's the case, we must refer back to a concept we discussed in the previous chapter — the idea that how we see our circumstances depends upon the things to which we compare them. That is, though assigning a score of "six" to each of our categories makes for a smaller-than-desirable diagram, the fact that everything's aligned tells us we're doing *okay* — and that brings us some relief.

However, when our helm consists of all "nines" and one "four," even though it's larger than that of the previous example, we'll usually feel worse about it. This happens for two reasons. The first is that a "four" looks far worse next to a "nine" than a "six" does alongside other "sixes." The second is that our uneven wheel means we're out of balance, and a helm with handles in all different places makes navigating troubled waters extremely difficult.

Now, how we relate this life-helm concept to yin and yang and my Hawaii story is in creating a system that compels us to revisit our drawings regularly. Though there are no hard and fast rules here, I recommend rescoring each section monthly and reviewing our categories and their respective sizes yearly. Once we've committed to such a process, we can follow through with it by putting these rescoring and resizing sessions on our calendars.

During these sessions, we'll look critically at our helms in hopes of making them more robust. We'll begin that task by first assessing their overall size and our satisfaction with that evaluation. Next, we'll determine which areas need the most work or attention. And, finally, we'll apply those determinations by devising ways to make our diagrams larger and more balanced.

For example, if we decide we aren't where we'd like to be in our love lives, we'll set goals for ourselves that bring us closer to such a place. For the single folks among us, this could mean committing to asking out one person in the next three weeks. For those already in intimate relationships, it could instead take the form of planning two special dates with our partners this month. And though the category may vary, the strategy won't — we'll apply this sort of thinking until we have a sound and actionable plan for raising and aligning all our sectors.

The reason it's critical we do such a thing is that it increases our odds of maintaining or rediscovering balance in several significant ways. First, it stops us from going years without checking in on ourselves and verifying that the direction we're sailing is still a desirable one. Second, it gives us an excuse to drop any obsessions we may have over where we are in life. After all, we have a trusted system in place, and we'll be okay if we just follow it. Finally, it keeps us focused on the progress we're making toward our goals rather than the abyss.

And while each of these three benefits is important in and of itself, when combined, they form a strategy that helps us straddle the line between yin and yang in a much more structured and effective way. That structure is crucial because it provides us with a map that leads us to the very places we hope to navigate. Without such a guiding force, we risk drifting over to rougher

AT RISK OF CAPSIZING

waters, where the waves whirl and tempt our boats to tip over, or worse — open the sea at its depths and expose our fleets to the vortex once more.

ONE WITH THE OCEAN

In the last twenty years, we've seen some of the largest companies in history rise to power. Over this period, present-day conglomerates, including Amazon, Facebook, and Google, grew from relatively obscure startups to market giants, garnering valuations north of a trillion dollars. Alongside these fast-growing behemoths, and thanks to the ubiquity of the internet and smartphones, came a multitude of other breakout successes as well — Airbnb, Lyft, Slack, Snapchat, and Uber — just to name a few.

For the most part, this explosion of valuations in the technology and consumer markets has been a positive thing, as it's inspired a new generation of passionate and driven go-getters. Now, with just a decent idea and an internet connection, budding entrepreneurs can pursue their own versions of the American dream by starting digitally-inclined companies. And, with a considerable amount of hard work and luck, they can make some serious cash on their creations.

After watching so many enterprises ascend from obscurity to riches in just a short span, countless Americans have incorporated businesses, launched products, and taken on the startup mindset themselves. This new societal trend has even infiltrated the highest ranks of our pop culture. Today, almost everywhere we turn, we see TV shows and podcasts about building and selling companies, and we hear increasingly popular, related terms like digital nomads and side hustles.

I've always been somewhat entrepreneurial myself, so I welcome and enjoy these changes — generally speaking. I love to see folks follow their passions, and I'd seldom tell anyone not to. In many ways, these broad social shifts indicate more and more folks are doing just that. However, that's not to say such developments don't also come with inherent downsides.

One of the largest of them is that a dogged, entrepreneurial pursuit can prohibit us from being present in our lives. When we aren't, such as when we worry about customers leaving negative reviews for our products online, we throw our bodies out of equilibrium by activating our internal survival mechanisms.[77] When those systems run for longer than they should — something that happens quite often for business owners and cofounders — we find ourselves in the metaphorical Strait of Messina, subjected to anxiety and depression once more.

As it pertains to the companies with which we opened this chapter, this same drawback-inspired logic tells us that while the biggest success stories in tech have given us hope that we, too, can create massive wealth for ourselves, they've also done something else — they've scared us. They've shown us that almost any industry can be upended overnight and that if we're not constantly innovating, our jobs and companies might be the next ones to get disrupted.

In turn, many organizations now operate like venture-backed startups, giving employees stock options and telling them to work harder than ever in hopes of outpacing competitors and unlocking massive paydays. If you've ever belonged to one of these businesses, I'm sure you've seen this sort of thing play out. Leaders push narratives and visions that may or may not be accurate, while team members wish the days away leading up to such dreams materializing. If we could just fast-forward to several years from now when our company finally sells, we tell ourselves, everything would be so much better.

While this kind of thinking can be inspiring and alluring, it too can strip us of our presence and prevent us from enjoying what we're doing on the job today. Making matters worse, thanks to our smartphones, email accounts, and messaging apps, we now take our tasks and conversations home with us, creating a workday that never really ends. These extended hours, combined with our future-based thinking, allow our jobs to permeate every aspect of our lives and cause us to lose sight of what we have outside of our careers.

What makes this loss of sight especially dangerous is that it invites one of depression's hallmarks back onto the scene: the feeling that life is flying by before our eyes. That is, when we constantly discard the moment in front of us, citing that everything would be better if we could just jump to one, three, or five years from now, we set ourselves up for a faceoff with that terrifying, hope-draining feeling.

HAPPINESS AND THE HEDONIC TREADMILL

Though our work lives are certainly one place we can fall prey to future-oriented thinking, the truth is, much of society is built upon this concept. It's not hard to find evidence supporting such an idea, either — all we have to do is turn on our TVs, phones, or computers and look at the advertisements that make their way onto the screen.

More often than not, the message these ads put forth is that we need the products they're pitching, and, until we buy them, we'll remain incomplete. These messages pull us out of the present moment once more by activating our fears of inadequacy. If we could only obtain all these products, then, just as if our companies got acquired, we'd finally be happy for the rest of our lives — right? Sadly, I don't quite think so.

The reason why is that our brains quickly adapt to new conditions and push us back toward our baseline levels of happiness shortly after we purchase new gadgets, join exclusive clubs, and take exotic vacations. In psychology, there's a term for this adaptation: *getting stuck on the hedonic treadmill*.[78] The quality of our lives improves, but our outlooks and emotions don't. This phenomenon can lead to what feels like a never-ending, wild goose chase for satisfaction.

Now, that's not to suggest happiness doesn't or can't exist — just that our society's model of how it comes about is a relatively broken one. As such, it's not surprising we're often shocked to hear that last year's lottery winner or the hottest new celebrity isn't happy or fulfilled, despite their newfound riches or success.[79] As puzzling or frustrating as these stories may sound, there's an explanation for this madness: happiness comes from within, not without. It emerges as a byproduct of continually striving and resting, doing the things we love, with the people we love, and enjoying both what we have today as well as what awaits us tomorrow.

Don't get me wrong, though. I'm also not suggesting money isn't important or can't contribute to the amount of joy we experience — I'm simply saying we should think twice before relying on it to solve all our problems. That's because, in classic, hedonic-treadmill-like fashion, the excitement we feel when we accumulate cash or consumer goods wanes over time. As such, we should relish that enthusiasm while we have it yet remain mindful that it might not last forever. If we don't, we may open ourselves up to some profound, negative emotions when it does disappear.

The two most common of them are disappointment and depression. These feelings often arise when we remember what we previously thought acquiring certain material goods would do for us. For example, when we say, "I always told myself this car or house would make me happy, and yet, here I am with them, still dissatisfied," we uncover a pain-producing mismatch between our past expectations and current realities.

Sometimes, we can escape such pain by getting back on our hedonic treadmills and setting our sights on the next item or experience we desire. Yet, while doing so can certainly lift our spirits in the short term, it rarely leads anywhere good in the long run. That's because, eventually, we'll rack up enough of those "I got what I wanted, and I'm still not happy" disappointments and become disillusioned by the entire process. That disillusionment can make us lose trust in the overall feasibility of happiness, which, in turn, stokes our hopelessness and causes the wormhole to the abyss to reopen.

To enter that hole, all we have to do is ask a higher-level, pessimistic life question as a result of our disillusionment. Examples of this include, "What's the point of even trying?" or, "Is this all there is?" Such questions rob us of our presence and extinguish our excitement for chasing worthy goals, both now and later on.

This sort of thinking applies to our entrepreneurial pursuits as well, as so many of us believe we'll finally be happy when we retire or achieve a particular milestone at work. Yet, the scary thing is, when we ultimately get to where we'd been trying to go all along, we sometimes find it's not as exciting as we thought it would be. This disparity can lead to the same sort of disillusionment and frustration we discussed a moment ago. And while those emotions are often quite demoralizing to experience, they too are not without a reasonable explanation.

That explanation is that presence and happiness are all about energy. When we engage in activities that inspire us, we're radiant, full of vigor, and distracted from our existential fears. However, when we stop performing those activities, be it because we retire, receive a promotion, or choose a new path in life, we lose the energy and excitement that come with them — and that's where the true standards for happiness and those of society clash and get us in trouble.

This exact problem is something that hip-hop mogul Russell Simmons discusses in his book, *Do You!*[80] In that work, Simmons recounts building and seeking buyers for his record label, Def Jam, and his clothing line, Phat Farm. In his mind, selling those companies would grant him huge paydays and massive boosts in happiness. After he sold them, however, he came to find that such exits were actually a letdown because handing his organizations over to someone else meant he could no longer perform the same work he'd been doing for years — the kind that inspired him and brought him energy daily.

Of course, it's easy to look at someone like Simmons and think to ourselves, "How could you possibly be unhappy? You're filthy rich!" But that would be missing the point. In reality, we now know it's energy and immersion that lead to joy — not necessarily money. When we ask *ourselves* such questions, when we set unrealistic expectations for our own happiness, we enter the wormhole to the abyss yet again. Seeing this possibility coming is one thing that helps both us and Simmons avoid such conundrum-related despair.

Now, none of this is to say entrepreneurialism and commercialism are inherently bad things. Even as someone who's become slightly disillusioned by them over the years, I still love many of the products and opportunities our consumer-centric society provides me. That said, I also understand how they sometimes become such significant parts of our lives that they tip our psychological scales out of balance. Thus, my intention with this discussion is not to suggest that the happiness game is unwinnable or that we shouldn't chase our desired aims but to remind us that we should always do so with a strong regard for moderation and the present moment. If we don't, we set ourselves up for a mental health disaster.

To further increase the likelihood of avoiding such a catastrophe, we must also do two other things. First, we must ensure the activities we pursue in our daily lives — be them working, training, studying, or caregiving — are inherently fulfilling or enjoyable for us and not just things we engage in for potential paydays down the road. If not, then, to the degree that we're able, we should seek to make changes.

For example, if we love creating marketing campaigns and are tired of our current role, we should search for a new position that best helps us cultivate that love — not one that seems boring but promises a big check in the future. If we opt for the latter, we may find ourselves uninspired until that check materializes and even more disappointed, later on, when we realize its ultimate arrival doesn't magically make us happy.

Second, we must create goals for ourselves that not only inspire us to get out of bed each morning but also allow us to retain enough of our focus to live in the moment. With this second strategy, we discover the concept of balance once more; these opposing forces hold one another in equilibrium and provide us harmony.

If we were to apply this same notion to the hypothetical aim of getting promoted to manager at our company, then doing so in the wrong fashion would look a lot like saying we won't be happy until we get there. However, if we have the same goal but approach it by telling ourselves we'll enjoy all the work we do during our time at the organization, no matter the role, we'll set ourselves up for a rewarding career and an engaged, present life at both the office and home.

THE BEWILDERING NATURE OF PRESENCE

One of the confusing things about presence is that there's a very thin line between being fully immersed in the moment and being stuck in our heads. When we're depressed, we're so entrenched in our suffering that we assume it means we're wholeheartedly attuned to the here and now. After all, if we weren't, how could we possibly be experiencing such pain?

This is the same sort of conundrum I faced on my 2018 trip to Europe, where I found myself deep in the bowels of my mind. As I sat in horror, sandwiched between the concepts of death and infinitude, I assumed I was more present than I'd ever been. In fact, I felt like I was practically drowning in that presence. As such, I couldn't see past my predicament, which only further convinced me of my assumptions.

Despite my focus, however, I failed to realize that what I was experiencing couldn't have been in-the-moment living because the sources of my pain were two things that weren't current realities. Neither death nor forever had anything to do with me sitting in an Airbnb in Europe with my friends. I'd somehow lost sight of that.

And while those things are undoubtedly spooky, they're future considerations at best, not present ones. The same goes for any other non-immediate, unsettling event or concept in our lives, be it the result of our upcoming, make-or-break sports tryout or the rise of artificial intelligence. Simply put, no matter the topic, if what we're fretting about isn't yet here today, then what we're engaging in, mentally, is both the complete opposite of presence and the real reason for our anguish.

By definition, it's impossible to be in our heads and the here and now simultaneously. When we're freaking out or rehashing far-off ideas, we may *feel* fully attuned to what's unfolding in front of us, but we most certainly are not. Regardless of what reassuring label we want to put on this sort of behavior, such as being practical or using logic, all we're really doing is hurtling ourselves toward another abyss — albeit one disguised as a calm wave. We must sail around that wave quickly. Otherwise, it may prove extremely dangerous.

The reason for that danger has everything to do with state management. As we recall, when we enter despair-filled states, we perceive our surroundings and what's happening in them not as they are but as reflections of our inner, temporarily pessimistic worlds. That means, instead of seeing opportunities, we see roadblocks, and instead of uncovering reasons to remain upbeat, we find reminders and reinforcers of our hopelessness.

Thus, this vortex-related danger to which I'm alluding is the frightening possibility that our transitory, negative perceptions drive us to make irreversibly damaging decisions — ones we wouldn't even consider in the right frame of mind. Examples of such things include experimenting with drugs and alcohol, gambling away our life savings, or committing heinous crimes.

Now, this is certainly not to downplay the seriousness of these situations, but how we get to the brink of such adverse behavior is by forgetting that our states and outlooks are virtually the same here. If we instead remembered this fact in real-time, we'd see the destructive actions we're considering as mere products of our current, wretched mindsets. Moreover, we'd actively seek to shift those mindsets, so we could change how we view such potential actions and conclude that they're not worth considering at all.

Another reason it can be so hard to detect when we're in our heads is that we're constantly jumping from our hearts to our minds at a moment's notice. One minute, we're blissfully playing cards with our siblings, and the next, we're reading terrifying TV headlines and plunging back into the gyre of despair without even realizing it. While this is an undoubtedly scary and challenging process to manage, it leads me to an interesting, related point that should help us better understand such struggles.

If we look up the word *psychosis* in the dictionary, we'll find a definition that refers to any severe mental disorder in which we become disconnected from reality. And while I admit that I may be taking things out of context here, I think it's important to state that, in some ways, when we're wholly *not present* in our lives, such as when gloom and doom pull us from our figurative card games, it's almost as if we've temporarily become psychotic.

Of course, that's a rather crude comparison, so I want to be careful not to make it sound like I'm belittling such a terrible condition — I'm certainly not. All I'm trying to do is put forth the point that head living and rumination are afflictions so debilitating they virtually qualify as diseases. If we want to avoid such disorders and stay present, we must diligently guard the doors of our minds.

Presence also goes further than simply assisting us in the mental health department, however. In fact, when you stop and think about it, it's not hard to see how here-and-now living was the very thing that helped us advance from one stage of our lives to the next. For example, when we worried about how we'd transition from middle school to high school or history class to basketball practice, we often became lost or frustrated. But when we instead slid into each moment and let our days take us wherever they'd planned, we usually leveled up with relative ease.

The same goes for the multitude of tasks we carry out regularly. When we dwell on the difficulty of running six miles in the hot summer sun, we stress ourselves out. But when we alternatively hit the streets at the drop of a dime and simply begin our workout, we reach that final mile marker without having encountered nearly as much anguish.

The point here is that, regardless of how we currently feel, if we can just get back to the moment in front of us and start moving again, we will, most of the time, ward off our negative emotions and end up in some pretty sweet places. Of course, that'll be much easier on some days than others, but, still, sounds good, right? That is, assuming we actually know how to find presence in our lives.

FINDING YOUR OWN FORM OF PRESENCE

Another confusing thing about presence is that it's a noun, not a verb. As such, it's not something in which we can directly participate. Unlike riding our bikes, listening to our favorite songs, or cleaning our rooms, we can't necessarily *do* presence. Nor can we head to the mall and purchase it from our favorite retailers. This elusiveness is one of the main reasons we sometimes find ourselves lacking it.

Instead, it arises naturally as a result of immersing ourselves in tasks and activities that excite, challenge, or relax us. Thus, another reason it can be so hard to come by is that, in our fast-paced, modern lives, we're often so busy we don't have time to engage in these pursuits. Yet, even when we do partake in them, we're usually so consumed by other distractions that we don't make room for this grounding force to emerge. That's a real problem because, to experience presence in all its glory, we must bring our full attention to such ventures.

One of the biggest of these distractions is our technology. It constantly keeps us *on* and disrupts us. These days, it's nearly impossible to turn around without seeing some kind of screen vying for our focus. And it's not just our phones I'm talking about — it's also our TVs, smartwatches, fitness trackers, tablets, and computers. Yes, all of these things help us stay more connected to the world, but they rarely help us get more connected with ourselves. Creating that internal kind is a requirement for presence.

Not that we can do it every hour of the day, but one tactic I utilize in my own life is to put my phone on do-not-disturb mode from time to time — most notably when I work out. To me, my exercise time is sacred. It's the short window when I try my hardest to get out of my head. If I'm going to the gym to work out, I also occasionally run into friends. Stopping and talking to them helps me find presence even more, as I temporarily forget about my digital distractions and worldly worries and settle into the conversation unfolding in front of me.

Most often, when we're struggling to sink into these immersive states, we're not adequately addressing such distractions. We must do so if we want to come back to the here and now. And while we can't always drop everything and go surfing for half the day, we can usually carve out thirty undistracted minutes and use that time to find the flow we've been craving. When we instead let our texts, emails, and notifications dictate our schedules, we subject ourselves to additional onslaughts of interruption and push ourselves even further from real, indivisible presence.

When it comes to discovering such a force, I never impose any particular strategy on anyone because that's not how presence works. We all enjoy different activities. What's engaging for me might not be for you. That's why my recommendation is simply to identify what those things are, then carry them out regularly.

Such pursuits could range from something simple, like discussing our passions with a friend or going to the beach, to something more complex, like taking kickboxing classes or editing videos on our computers.

The only requirement I have for this process is that, when seeking presence, we actually allow ourselves to discover it by minimizing or eliminating our external interferences. During these brief periods of engagement, all that matters is our connection to whatever it is we're doing. Once we let go of the chaos in our personal lives, we'll find we can better slip into the moment in front of us. And, once we're in that moment, I think we'll see our continuous inner dialogues of fear and hopelessness quiet down a bit.

And though it may, at first, seem like delaying the inevitable to push our worries aside for a few minutes, such thinking ignores the fact that when we change our state, our troubles change, too. Sometimes, they do so just enough, or for just long enough, for us to see them in new, more hopeful fashions. That allows us, even if only momentarily, to pull ourselves out of our doomsday-inclined minds.

The more we do such a thing, the better we'll get at doing it, and the greater we'll understand its importance and effectiveness. For, as scary as some of the events and circumstances on the horizon may appear, those things are not current-day truths. Our only guaranteed reality is what's in front of us right now. When we realize this fact and live by it, we give

ONE WITH THE OCEAN

ourselves a chance to reclaim our vessels from the throes of the vortex and move back to a much more empowering state of mind.

OFF COURSE AND RUDDERLESS

Up to this point in the book, we've looked at countless ways depression manifests in our lives. We've seen how our internal states of fear and anxiety can drive us into despair and how a myriad of stressors in our external environments bring about those states. And, most importantly, we've deconstructed the abyss and familiarized ourselves with the fashions in which it operates.

However, one thing we haven't done — at least not in full — is investigate how the entire mental health ocean functions below the surface. In other words, though we've determined what *we* sometimes do to cause our depression to appear, we haven't finalized our discussion on how *the world*, in general, can shepherd us into carrying out melancholy-promoting actions, behaviors, and thought patterns.

One of the most common ways it does so is through its norms, rules, and customs. We call the combination of these things *culture*. When we boil that term down, we see that the behavior-shaping guidance it provides stems from our shared values — the things we collectively feel are important. Thus, in a sense, what we deem significant ultimately directs what we can and can't do or who we should and shouldn't be.

Of course, these days, it's rare that anyone forces us to adhere to a specific collection or combination of values. That's the beautiful thing about the free world, after all — we can, to some degree, choose our paths in life. But there's still a potential problem with this concept of value adoption, and, no, it's not coercion. Instead, it's something slightly more insidious.

Namely, it's the inverse: When no one forces us to adhere to a particular set of values, we often blindly follow the unspoken rules of civilization and let them lead us to despair without even realizing it. Thus, when looking at our culture, the question I ask myself is, "What are the specific, society-wide values we've taken on throughout our lives that have similarly led us astray?"

By my estimations, there are three that stand out most: independence, money, and certainty. When we place too much emphasis on these ideas, we guide ourselves into the perspectives, behaviors, and outcomes that put us at significant risk for depression.

And while it typically takes years, if not decades, to change societal values across the board, we all get to choose which ones we want to prioritize in our own lives. Once we start edging toward more empowering ones that better support our mental health, we'll find that we fall into the aforementioned, insidious abysses far less frequently. So, with that in mind, let's discuss the first of our three destructive values — independence.

BECOMING INTERDEPENDENT

Starting in our youth, our elders teach us to strive for excellence. In the classroom, professors tell us that if we work and study hard, we'll get good grades, land prestigious jobs, and score the coolest homes and gadgets. And, in the athletic realm, coaches encourage us to rack up points and personal records so our peers will respect us and colleges will recruit us.

While there's nothing wrong with aspiring for personal greatness, the ways we bring that greatness about can sometimes be harmful in the long run. One example of this is how our traditional blueprints for success instruct us to push others aside in pursuit of our own accomplishments. In competitive environments such as the classroom and the playing field, scarcity mindsets rally us against our cohorts. These same mindsets ask us, "Why would I let my teammate win the MVP award when I want it for myself?"

Now, before I risk sounding like an outright denouncer of personal achievement, let me take a step back. After all, my aim here is not to advocate for participation medals or suggest that we shouldn't work hard to make names for ourselves. It's just to say that, if we're not careful, our quests for success can compel us to value independence so highly we forget the importance of those around us.

You've seen or heard this self-reliant outlook in action before. Countless hit songs over the years have declared it. They're the ones proclaiming, "I'm independent. I bought my car and house all on my own, and I sure as heck don't need anyone besides myself to be happy and triumphant."

Though most of these songs are fun to listen to, the problem with them, and their accompanying mindsets, is that they paint a false portrait of reality. There are two things I'm referring to when I make such a claim. First, success and independence rarely coexist. Second, if we value the latter too highly, we're setting ourselves up for a showdown with isolation and depression — not happiness.

If you've ever watched one of the many popular awards shows on television, you'll understand this first point quite well already. Upon receiving Grammys for their talent and hard work, even the hottest bands and pop stars thank their producers, engineers, songwriters, managers, record labels, friends, family, and so on. The reason they do such a thing is they realize that, without all those people, they likely wouldn't be on stage in the first place.

As it pertains to the second point, holding independence in too high a regard can force us to distance ourselves from others in both subtle and more pronounced ways. Over time, such isolation-fostering actions can spiral upon themselves, secluding us further, reducing the amount of support we have, and creating additional stress in our lives. Sadly, regardless of how much we've achieved or earned, that solitude, and the despair that often comes with it, are tough obstacles to surmount.

One of the reasons these troubles repeatedly emerge in our lives is that our society's overpromotion of autonomy tends to push us into such independence-inspired behaviors without us noticing. What that means for us is we must remember to stay mindful of how highly we're prioritizing this value on both a conscious and subconscious level. Moreover, when we feel it's negatively affecting our mental health, we must seek balance by going out of our way to connect with others.

As we saw in the chapter entitled "Scylla, Meet Charybdis," not having those connections can set off our brain's emergency alert systems just like that of real, physical threats. When those systems repeatedly work overtime, they produce all sorts of unwanted side effects, including hopelessness and poor long-term health. This morbid conclusion is something that Harvard University's seventy-five-year-long study on adult development shows us as well.[81] Put plainly, isolation and loneliness kill.

So, if a quest for personal independence isn't all that likely to lead us to positive mental health outcomes, what should we instead seek and prioritize? I'd suggest *interdependence*. With this new value as a north star, we'll not only build more robust support systems that help keep us afloat when the abyss beckons, but we'll also gain a much-needed first line of defense against that terrifying foe.

Of course, becoming interdependent is a rather vague concept. That's why I want to quickly cover the most reliable way by which we can integrate such a value into our lives. Though that strategy — building trusting relationships — is also a bit nebulous, as well as borderline obvious, it's one that research suggests is strongly correlated with happiness.[82]

While these relationships may be romantic, they can also be platonic, familial, or work-related. In deep, caring ones, we learn to lean on one another when difficulties and challenges arise.

And though it can be daunting to think about finding more good friends and building stronger bonds, we must remember, such a journey starts with the first step; as long as we're there for the people in our circles, strong connections will eventually emerge.

It doesn't matter whether we're talking about coworkers, neighbors, or family members, either. If we continue to put in the effort with them, be it by persevering through project deadlines together or calling each other weekly, we'll eventually look up and realize we've established ties with individuals on whom we can rely. These folks support us and help us through the stresses of our lives.

Though I could certainly go on with the countless methods by which we could seek interdependence, what I think might be more appropriate is a quick conclusion on the subject. After all, as an adult, I'm sure you can brainstorm plenty of other ways, specific to your own life, to get more involved in your family, company, or community. As such, I'll leave the discovery of those means to you and instead focus on our main takeaway for this section: we all need people on whom we can depend. As the previously mentioned Harvard study shows, togetherness isn't just wired into our nervous systems — it's also a much better predictor of happiness than personal achievement.[83]

Unfortunately, society rarely echoes such vital wisdom. Instead, it suggests that relying on anyone besides ourselves is a weakness. In reality, that idea isn't just dangerous for our mental health — it's also wrong. Leaning on others is a strength. It shows we're not afraid to open up and be vulnerable. When we defy this misinformed societal logic, reach out, and establish bonds with others, we not only push our seclusion back into the depths of the sea, but we also construct a life raft we can jump into the next time we're not feeling like ourselves.

REPRIORITIZING MEANING

It's not long after we've begun our journeys toward independent achievement that we set our sights on money — and lots of it. It's another major part of our social fabric and conditioning. As we grow up, we glean from movies, TV shows, and various role models that accumulating wealth will help us become free and exceedingly happy.

Just like our quests for individual accomplishment, there's nothing inherently wrong with trying to pad our bank accounts. We all have to put food on the table, pay our bills, and support ourselves and our families. That's why, similarly to the previous section, I'm not suggesting we abandon this second value altogether — just that we be careful with it.

The main reason for such caution is that money isn't as correlated with joy as we might think. In fact, countless research studies over the years have shown us that once we approach a particular salary figure, each additional dollar we earn stops providing us an incremental happiness boost. According to one of those studies, a 2018 trial conducted by Purdue University and University of Virginia psychologists, that figure lies somewhere between $60,000 and $95,000, not accounting for inflation.[84]

Thus, if we're still chasing checks in the name of joy once we've earned beyond that range, we're playing a game we're unlikely to win.

Of course, that's not to suggest we can't aim for six figures or more. Nor is it to say that a few broadly-based research projects understand the details of our financial situations and what a particular sum of money might mean to us. Still, when we look at the data at a high level, it's not hard to see its overall point: more money doesn't always mean more happiness. Sometimes, it just means further disappointment or disillusionment.[85]

When I first came across studies like these, I was dumbfounded. I'd always believed money and happiness were intimately intertwined, up to even the highest levels of wealth. As such, it seemed apparent to me these researchers didn't know what they were saying. However, as the years went by, I learned to appreciate their wisdom a bit more.

When you think about it, that $60,000 to $95,000 range, roughly speaking, is the point at which most people become capable of living on their own, paying their bills, and even saving a little cash. For us, a steady salary in that range removes some of our worldly pressures, which allows us to stop worrying so much about making ends meet and reduces the amount of anxiety we regularly experience.

Above that $95,000 mark, however, we typically find we aren't decreasing our stress levels all that much further — we're just accumulating newer or more luxurious forms of the things we already have. These upgrades rarely provide us the same lasting boosts we received when we bought our first versions of them long ago.

Now, if these insights sound slightly familiar, that means you were paying attention in the last chapter during our discussions surrounding the hedonic treadmill. Nice job. Even though we've covered that topic at length already, our salary-centric conversations present us with an opportunity to drive home an essential conclusion on it.

That conclusion goes a little something like this: Society often pushes us to chase the next carrot in front of us, claiming it will be the thing that makes us happy once and for all. As a result, we usually believe such notions and do just that. However, when we finally acquire what we thought would complete us, we sometimes find we don't feel nearly as good as expected.

This discrepancy leads us to one of three choices. We can jump back on our metaphorical treadmills by chasing more money or consumer goods, we can sail into the wormhole to the abyss by asking ourselves if anything will ever satisfy us, or we can instead undertake tasks and ventures that excite us and help us cultivate purpose.

While the first two options are certainly tempting, the last choice is the only viable one, for it's the only selection that doesn't eventually end in a whirlpool. So, despite my long-winded way of getting there, this is what I mean when I say we should deprioritize our pursuit of financial aims; we should seek a healthy balance of affluence and the activities that bring us the most meaning in the short and long run.

Without question, however, the blanket term *meaning* is quite nebulous — much like some of the other concepts we've covered in this chapter. So, for simplicity's sake, let's assume it refers to the uplifting feeling we experience when we follow our hearts or make a positive impact on the world or those around us. Some of the quickest routes to this feeling are our passions, missions, and dreams — the subjects and activities that call to our souls and help us come alive. The same ones that some folks argue are our true purposes on Earth, insulators from the inevitable tragedies of life, and how we connect with a higher power.[86]

Of course, how we each seek meaning varies because we're all interested in different things. Regardless, there are two main reasons why cultivating *any* form of it is so important in life. The first is that meaningful activities help us become more present and engaged. And, second, those same tasks are the exact, fulfillment-bringing ones we'd be participating in if money were no object.

Just think about that last point for a minute. When we accumulate wealth, it's not our little green pieces of paper that bring us joy — at least not directly. Heck, most of the time, we never even see our cash — it simply enters and exits our checking accounts digitally. Instead, it's the items and experiences we'll obtain with those bills and the feelings we believe such things will provide us that fuel our search for prosperity.

Or, to put it more directly, we chase money because we think it'll eventually lead to happiness. And while it certainly can to a degree, it's not the most efficient route for us to get to that pleasant place; sometimes, we need to go straight to the source instead. We do that via our favorite pastimes, creative endeavors, nights spent with friends and family, and contributions to the less fortunate. These acts are the ones that have no end, as they're destinations in and of themselves. Such passion-laced deeds provide more meaning than money ever could.

Since much of this logic hearkens back to our previous discussions on presence, I won't risk repeating myself too much further here. However, I do want to touch upon one more related idea before we close this section. That idea is that when we don't regularly pursue meaning, we make ourselves vulnerable to another familiar origin of despair — the feeling that life is flying by before our eyes. Here's what I'm referring to with such a statement.

We all have specific things we'd like to do or accomplish before leaving this world. These are our bucket list items and most meaningful personal projects. However, because we spend so much time in our lives figuring out how to survive and pay the bills, we often push these things off to a later date.

When we're young, this doesn't seem like such a big deal. After all, we have decades ahead of us. Yet, as we get older, we see the clock ticking. As the years march on and we realize we either haven't taken action on these meaningful projects or have squandered the opportunity to complete them altogether, we open ourselves up to a special kind of loss — the feeling that we took our time on Earth for granted. More often than not, this perceived loss is the very force behind the sentiment that life is racing by and the despair associated with it.

Thus, to insulate ourselves against this sneaky form of gloom, we should get to work on these projects as soon as possible. That way, even if our days do go by quickly, we can at least look back and say, "I did it just the way I wanted to. I have no regrets."

Though our newfound balance of money and passion-filled ventures certainly helps us make such reassuring statements and cultivate purpose, there's another vital factor at play in our meaning equation. That factor is faith, and it's the final replacement value we're going to cover.

BALANCING CERTAINTY AND FAITH

When I was a kid, my family and I practiced Catholicism. We went to mass each week, and my brother and I regularly attended Sunday school. Our parents were never too strict about our faith. They merely sought to raise us with good values so we could make informed decisions about how we wanted to live.

However, in 2002, after *The Boston Globe* uncovered the Catholic church's history of sexual abuse, our family started going to mass far less frequently. Though none of the priests in our parish participated in the atrocities themselves, it still felt wrong to affiliate with an organization that hid such horrible and hypocritical behavior. As such, after my confirmation, we quickly fell out of the community in full.

As the subsequent years passed, and I graduated from college and moved to the city, it dawned on me that I didn't know just what I believed anymore. Yes, I still felt our journeys on Earth are sacred and that we're all connected on some level. But when I thought about it, I didn't have good answers to the more significant and existential questions about life. That scared me.

Part of the reason for this uncertain outlook was that I hadn't been to church in several years. Another major factor was that I was now part of a secular global economy. Everywhere I turned, from the internet to the workplace, I saw yet another reminder of how business, money, and hedonism had transformed faith and spirituality into second-class citizens. Though I didn't quite know what it was about such messages that made me uneasy, I knew *something* didn't feel right.

Yet, it wasn't for another few years — during my 2018 bout of depression, to be exact — that this internal conflict reared its ugly head. In the depths of my despair, I pondered my big, existential questions in earnest: where we come from, the meaning of life, and where we go when we perish. Still without good answers to such questions, I spun the wheels in my mind and fell further and further into helplessness.

As I worked through that battle and inched toward recovery, I realized two crucial, faith-related things. The first was, shockingly, that I didn't have much of it at the time. The second was that we all need a reasonable dose of it to be mentally healthy.

When it comes to that second point, I don't mean we need to subscribe to a particular religion or set of teachings. Nor am I going to pitch you on one. I simply mean that if we want to avoid the abyss, we must have faith in something larger than ourselves and our problems; we must believe in ideas and concepts that help each of us find peace.

One thing that guided me to these conclusions was reading a book I mentioned earlier — *Maps of Meaning* by Jordan Peterson. In that mega-work, Peterson declares that the collapse of faith in our value systems leads to depression, turmoil, and existential anxiety.[87] Or, in other words, when we destroy the organizations that provide answers to life's most profound questions and stop believing in the things that supply us with meaning and purpose, it's not long before we find ourselves lost, aimless, and overwhelmed with fear.

Now, I'm no historian, but I think it's safe to say our world is a bit less faith-based, overall, than it was in previous generations. That's not to suggest no one has faith anymore, however, just that our society no longer revolves around it like it once did. Though there are several factors behind such a shift, the most influential, in my mind, are the rise of science and our never-ending hunt for certainty.

As human beings, we crave to know the answers to all of our questions, to understand where we're heading and what tomorrow will bring. This craving, when left unchecked, becomes a key catalyst of several mental illnesses, especially anxiety, as it pushes us to obsess over important, upcoming events in our lives and, counterintuitively, strips us of what little confidence we have in regard to them.

One of the reasons we love science, then, is it's a great place to channel some of these inquiries, worries, and doubts. By simply starting with a question, then experimenting and analyzing, we can generate answers to some of our most pressing curiosities.

As you can probably tell, I'm a big believer in science myself. Among other things, I love how the conclusions we draw from our research can help improve the lives of others. Without it, the psychiatric world wouldn't have made all the discoveries it did over the last century, and I likely wouldn't have been able to write this book. But still, that doesn't mean science isn't without its limitations. Here's what I mean by that.

The scientific process works very well when the subject at hand or the object of our questioning is measurable, testable, and capable of producing evidence or proof — case in point, running a research study on the efficacy of antidepressant drugs. However, as great a tool as it is, it's not the right one for all of our predicaments. That's because not everything we encounter is tangible, observable, and knowable. But that's where faith comes in.

Faith is both the opposite and the complement of science. It's a belief in the invisible, regardless of the evidence currently at our disposal. When we have it, we allow ourselves to put our fears down and stop worrying all the time since we know they'll eventually, and somehow, resolve themselves.

In truth, we need both this grounding force *and* science. To see why the former is so necessary, despite our societal shortage of it, let's look at four of the concepts we've previously discussed through a new, faith-curved lens. The first of them is none other than depression itself.

Without science, we wouldn't know nearly as much about the disease as we do. And yet, when we're actually going through a bout of melancholy, science can only take us so far. Yes, it can provide us medication, insights, and prognoses, and all of those things can be extremely helpful. But what science can't offer is hard evidence that our specific bout will soon conclude. For that kind of thing, we need faith.

When we possess it, we trust in that which is not yet here today. That means we're confident things will get better, even if we don't understand how. When we lose that trust, we focus solely on the evidence, or lack thereof, before us. In the middle of a mental typhoon, that typically only makes the waves grow taller. That's why faith is so crucial. It permits us to look past our current reality and set our sights on the calmer waters ahead.

The second example to which I want to apply this line of thinking is climate change. Without science, we likely wouldn't have any idea that the ways most of us live are harming the planet. Nor would we have access to the technological breakthroughs that may someday allow us to reverse and overcome such damage. However, one thing science can't do is declare whether or not we'll conquer this terrifying foe. Only faith can do that.

If we look at what we know about the subject today, we see there's no hard evidence supporting the claim that we'll clean up our planet and ensure the long-term survival of our species. So, what are we supposed to do about that? Just live in misery while we wait for the end to come? Of course not. Instead, we plot and plan, strive and strategize, and hold onto our belief that we'll find a way through, despite not currently having proof — because that's what you do when you have faith.

The last concepts to which I want to apply this sort of thinking are the ones that opened this section: the meaning of our lives and our ultimate fate. Now, I know this kind of discussion is unsettling, so if you don't feel like getting existential for a moment, then, by all means, skip ahead to the next section. For those of us who want to dig deeper, however, let's move forward.

If we listen to science, we realize there aren't many great explanations on these two topics just yet. In fact, a few of the conclusions it does offer are pretty dark. For example, some researchers suggest we're just lines of computer code in a simulation or bits of space dust floating through a random universe. Good grief. I imagine you now understand what Jordan Peterson was talking about when he warned of the collapse of faith in society's value hierarchy. The pain associated with that collapse, as well as science's shortcomings regarding these subjects, show us why we need such a stabilizing force in our lives.

With it in hand, we gain another powerful tool — just like science — that we can use to navigate many of the challenges we encounter. But, of course, the tricky thing about these tools is knowing which one to leverage and when. That's why I want to make our current choice as clear as possible: When it comes to our profound life questions, we must look past science, admit what we don't know, and hand our uncertainties, fears, and doubts over to a higher power. We must trust that there's order, purpose, and an uplifting explanation to it all — even if we can't prove that just yet.

Though making such trusting assertions without hard evidence to support them can undoubtedly seem irrational, we must remember we do something similar, albeit on more minor scales, all the time. For example, we continue to play hard when our intramural teams are down twenty points, and we keep looking for new employment opportunities even after striking out for months. The reason we do such things is we know that, despite not having proof that they will, these scenarios can, and sometimes do, turn themselves around — and that mindset exemplifies what it means to have faith.

Yet, it also raises a question: If we can have faith in the outcome of a game, then can't we have it in regard to just about anything? The answer, as we've seen throughout this section, is yes. There's a reason for that. Though I'm primarily using the word *faith* in the spiritual sense here, it can also refer to our confidence in a particular person, object, or idea. And, when we really get down to it, each of us holds many such convictions — good, bad, or indifferent — all of which influence how we see the world and our experiences in it.

Now, that leads me to two final questions — the most important ones in this chapter. First, does what you believe about yourself, your life, and the world support your mental health or undermine it? Second, do those beliefs give you a solid foundation to lean on when facing challenges and difficulties?

If your answer to either of those questions is *no*, I'd like to remind you of an understated yet fitting takeaway from our deliberations on intentional ignorance: We get to decide what we believe in life. More importantly, we can believe anything we want, so long as it helps us find meaning, provides us with empowering ways of getting through challenges, and doesn't harm others. In fact, not only can we, but, I'd argue, we *must*, as it's one of the best ways to protect our vessels from the maelstrom.

And while it may sound peculiar or wrong to update or replace our convictions, I think the stranger thing would be to hold on to ones that no longer serve us. As such, when the time comes to evaluate our options, we should dismiss those that set us up for confusion and despair and adopt the ones that help each of us live more stable, inspired lives.

The reason spirituality-geared beliefs bring us such stability and inspiration is that they give us a strong base of meaning in the higher realm that then allows us to turn our focus toward more worldly, day-to-day pursuits of purpose. The same ones that help us cultivate energy and find presence.

When we lack that meaning, as well as faith-based assurances and explanations to the most unanswerable questions in life, we put ourselves at exceptionally high risk for despair. Sure, maybe a more abstract kind of risk, but still, a formidable one nonetheless. Yet, despite such potential grief, there is a way out. That way is by doubling down on our convictions and visions for the future and letting them carry us from even the roughest of storms.

LIVING OUR VALUES

Throughout this chapter, we scrutinized some of the personal and societal values that cause us the most mental health trouble. And while I'm sure it sounded like I was veering from the depression discussion a bit at times, there was a purpose behind that detour. It was to highlight how the values we prioritize, on both an individual and collective level, eventually creep into every area of our lives and influence our emotions, thoughts, and behaviors — despair-related ones included.

That purpose also leads me to two conclusions I've wanted to make throughout this entire, values-based discussion. The first is that happiness, or at the very least, fulfillment, is a byproduct of ignoring the societal values that don't serve us and wholeheartedly living out our own. That is, so long as they're good ones.

The second conclusion goes a little something like this: Because society's values have a considerable influence over our lives, it's not always our fault when we become depressed. Sometimes, our culture simply leads us to believe the wrong things, and, as a result, we wind up in some less than desirable places. However, even though we're not always the ones to blame for our despair, we're still responsible for taking care of ourselves and doing something about it. That something could be changing our routines or thought patterns, getting ourselves to the doctor, or opening up about our struggles to a loved one.

One of the main ways society ushers us down this path is by pushing us into tasks and careers that don't align with our interests and passions. Despite promises that they'll bring us great joy, such activities and plans typically only cause us to feel stuck, and that emotion makes finding happiness and fulfillment very challenging.

This sentiment is something that author Marianne Williamson discusses in her book, *Healing the Soul of America*. In it, she notes that most of us just want to go to sleep because we're depressed.[88] And can you guess why many of us feel that way? Because we're not doing what our souls are calling us to do.

Instead, we're hustling for wages so we can keep up with the Joneses. And while our paychecks may put stylish outfits in our closets and money in our savings accounts, they'll never silence the voices in our ears saying, "Life's too short to be dissatisfied. Don't let your gifts go to waste. Wake up and share them with the world. Live."

Of course, sometimes we have no choice but to work jobs we don't love. There's nothing to be ashamed of in that. However, if we're to sail such a route, we might as well use it as a means to some other fulfilling end, such as paying for our child's dream of going to dance school.

That way, we'll derive meaning and purpose from our careers, which will protect us from falling into these associated pits of misery so easily. The same goes for jobs that help us create that meaning directly, either through assisting others or expressing ourselves. As long as there's no excess of stress in any other area of our lives, these roles will usually insulate us from such agony as well.

Now, none of this is to say that finding meaning is necessarily a straightforward, black-and-white process. Nor that the decisions related to cultivating it are always easy to make. It's just to state that if we don't put ourselves back at the helm and sail under the power of good values, we'll never reach our desired, fulfillment-granting port.

The reason this conclusion is so vital is that it's unlikely, at best, society will ever give us that power. Instead, it'll continue to push the wrong values and breed classes of well-intentioned but misguided souls — ones destined for significant pain down the road. This theme is something we see recur time and time again in the media. I don't even need to remind you of how many stories come forth, on a regular basis, of multimillionaires, moguls, and chart-topping musicians who suffer from addiction, substance abuse, and mental illness, despite seemingly having it all.

There's an interesting yet terrifying reason many of these people feel the way they do: disillusionment. Here's what I'm getting at with that assertion. At the suggestion of society's values, they chase fame, fortune, freedom, and fancy designer goods. And yet, when they finally gain that freedom or score those coveted items, they sometimes realize such things don't actually make them happy — and never even could've. That painful realization then further distracts them from the true sources of joy they've been missing all along: their own abandoned values.

Worse yet, by getting where they were hoping to go, these same folks lose the grounding and distracting forces associated with struggling, striving, and dreaming. As a result, they find themselves in a special kind of hell — one that's eerily comfortable and provides little hope of a more promising future. After all, they've pulled the curtain back on that future, and now, it doesn't look so appealing.

This sort of dissonance is incredibly hard to overcome. It represents a catastrophic loss — one that reopens the wormhole to the abyss. Without the striving-associated distraction these folks once had, they wind up deep in their heads. In that scary place, they sometimes ask the most dangerous sorts of questions, such as what the meaning of life is, whether or not they'll just struggle forever, and if the games of happiness and fulfillment are even winnable ones in the first place.

What only makes these situations worse is that these celebrities' followers rarely understand their plight, either. As such, fans gossip, text, and tweet about these people and how ungrateful or spoiled they are when, in fact, that might not be the whole story. In reality, and below the surface, many of these lost souls are simply experiencing the daunting downsides of lifestyles predicated upon hollow values.

This cycle of disillusionment, misunderstanding, gossip, and despair typically only continues until such people drown themselves in drugs and alcohol or check into rehab. And even then, fans sometimes scoff, "All that money and fame, and they threw it away like that? What a waste." If these followers only knew how dangerous disempowering values and "I'll be happy when" statements were, maybe they'd more readily see the burden these people bear.

Yet, it's not just celebrities who face this sort of gloom. We, too, can get to where we want to go in life only to find that the outcome is not the one we'd envisioned.[89] If we're not careful, that discrepancy can lead to the return of our old friend, Mr. Swirly Abyss. And while there isn't always one simple action we can take to escape such a foe, there is a way to avoid him, and it's basing our lives on the sorts of values we've talked about and pursuing goals we find inherently rewarding.

BURIED TREASURE

As discussed in the previous chapter, when we adopt wholesome values and pursue the activities, goals, and lifestyles associated with them, we reduce our risk of experiencing unwanted afflictions such as disillusionment and depression. That discussion now leads us to an important question: If we already know what those values are, or, at the very least, if we could come up with some fairly quickly, what's stopping us from pursuing such empowering objectives and ways of life? The answer, much of the time, is trauma.

In the general sense, trauma refers to deeply disturbing experiences and the intense psychological distress we encounter during them.[90] These events are the most significant and emotionally charged ones of our lives, such as abuses, abandonments, incidents of violence, car accidents, natural disasters, wars, life-threatening illnesses, and so on.

It's tough to put into words just how difficult it is to go through one of these experiences. Yet, despite the magnitude of that difficulty, it might not even be the worst feature of such occurrences. Arguably, that title instead goes to what trauma does to us in the long run; quite often, it shatters our senses of security and reality, throws us off course, and alters our entire journey in life.

While there are many ways trauma can do such a thing, one of the main ones is via a condition known as Post-Traumatic Stress Disorder (PTSD). This affliction is a long-term one marked by an inability to recover from whatever it is that sparked our suffering in the first place.[91] Though it's typically associated with soldiers returning from war, it affects a wide range of people who've been through all sorts of troubling experiences.

The most common symptoms associated with PTSD are nightmares and flashbacks — sufferers resee the petrifying things they went through over and over again in their minds. But it's not just the mind that relives these calamities. The body does, too; with these recollections, our nervous systems often return to fight-flight-or-freeze mode, even when there's no physical threat in front of us.

When we boil it down, we see that these replayings of past terrors, and PTSD in general, are essentially our brains' ways of saying, "That event nearly broke me. I don't know what to do with it." This is why we frequently hear of soldiers reliving the horrors of war long after they've returned from battle. What they witnessed was so distressing, their minds still can't make sense of it, weeks, months, or years later. As such, they constantly revisit it, hoping to one day process it and let go of it for good.

As if these sufferers don't have it bad enough, PTSD can become such a powerful force in their lives that it prevents them from functioning normally. In these situations, trauma-based memories and fears turn simple tasks like leaving the house or socializing into overwhelming, dread-laced ordeals. These nagging interferences can then lead to substance abuse, strained relationships, and feelings of hopelessness. And what do we get when we combine any number of those things for a long enough time? You guessed it: depression.[92]

REVISITING RUDDERLESSNESS

Though not all of us have been through the ravages of war or abuse, many of us have experienced our own forms of trauma. After all, its definition isn't exactly hard and fast — anything that horrifies *us*, in particular, will fit the bill. In other words, since our bodies all work slightly differently, what's terrifying for some might not be for all. But who are we to judge, and what does that matter, anyway? We don't define what terror is — the psyche of the person experiencing it does.

No matter what kinds of trauma we've been through — and, yes, the data suggests most of us have been through *some* — we too can become debilitated by it if we're not cautious.[93] The tricky thing is, many of us are indeed careful with our traumas, just not in the right way. That is, instead of finding empowering outlets for such distress, we tend to keep it to ourselves, hole up, and hope it will eventually stop tormenting us. Moreover, and most importantly, we avoid the activities and behaviors that could potentially reignite the flames of our harrowing pasts.

Though this strategy isn't without its good intentions — and, trust me, I realize just how valiant those leviathan-fighting aims are — it typically does more harm than good in the long run.

Here's why. At first, such an approach seems like it'll help us experience the least amount of pain possible. But, over time, it morphs into something that stops us from progressing in life.

The logic associated with a strategy of this flavor might sound something like, "Why would I step back out into the world and risk facing countless reminders of my anguish? Why would I subject myself to getting hurt yet again? Wouldn't it be safer to just hide out in my bedroom?" Though we all need to do whatever works best for us, and while that sometimes means temporarily holing ourselves up in the comfort of our homes, we can't stay there forever — not physically nor mentally. Unfortunately, many of us still do.

No, I'm not saying we actually sit in our bedrooms for the rest of our days — just that we continue to live as if we're still in those rooms long after we've emerged from them. We rejoin the world, but we shelter ourselves psychologically. We live cautiously and in a detached fashion, not incessantly suffering, but certainly not thriving either. Furthermore, and worst of all, we take our pain and hide it deep inside ourselves, hoping it will never resurface again.

And while this approach may very well be the best or only way we know of dealing with our agony, I must remind us: It's not a healthy means of getting by in the world. That's because we can't bury our anguish without also disconnecting from the meaningful subjects behind it — the ones that, if we're honest with ourselves, could, one day, help us get back to normal, healthy functioning. In real life, this burying can take many forms. For example, after a history of abuse from significant others, we may swear off relationships altogether. Or, after a colossal, embarrassing meltdown during a singing contest, we may give up our lifelong aspirations of becoming musicians.

Of course, either of these reactions would be natural and understandable given our distress. Yet, even though that's the case, neither one sets us up for lasting success or sustained mental health. Why? Because just as we saw in the previous paragraph, when we disengage from these kinds of pain, we also detach from our goals, our dreams, and the parts of ourselves we need in order to flourish. Without such wellsprings of hope and joy, we eventually lose our will to keep moving forward.

What makes this process even more sinister is that this sort of thing rarely happens consciously or quickly. Typically, we encounter so much pain or endure such a long string of hurts in a vital area of our lives that we slowly start to see that which could bring us joy as things that will only ever cause us despair. That pain then gradually changes us until we're months or years past our initial experiences of trauma, dissatisfied with where we are in life, and completely unsure as to why.

Unfortunately, this ship is one that rarely rights itself — at least not without an *aha* moment on our part. Worse yet, getting to such breakthroughs takes time, introspection, and the safe unpacking of our trauma with trusted therapists. However, the good news is, many of us do eventually uncover such insights. And, despite the pain required to reach them, that's a huge step forward.

BURIED TREASURE

One of the biggest of those breakthroughs is the same concept we've been alluding to throughout this section: Though seemingly unrelated, our trauma and depression are often intimately connected. When we finally make that realization, we provide ourselves an opportunity to move past our pain by seeing that our buried hurts were actually buried treasures all along. It's at this point we stand the chance of finding some serious gold, so long as we're willing to carry out the difficult task of digging for it.

OPENING UP THE CHEST

Now, of course, I need to be cautious when I make such glorifying statements; I'm certainly not attempting to put trauma on a pedestal here. Nor am I trying to claim that all forms of it have direct and opposite responses associated with them that will always get us back on track in life. I'm just saying that pain can send us wildly off course at times. As such, if we're not willing to confront it, we might not right the ship for quite a while — and that's true of both our battles with the abyss as well as the countless other challenges we face on our maritime adventures.

To put it another way, to accomplish whatever it is we desire — whether overcoming depression or getting promoted at work — we inevitably have to put ourselves out there and risk encountering hardship and disappointment. If we want to find the paradise islands, we have to brave the treacherous conditions of the open ocean. Sure, we could always avoid all forms of that risk by keeping our boats at the docks, but doing so would mean never allowing ourselves the opportunity to find the treasure.

Funny enough, we sometimes do such a thing anyway because we think not using our ships means they'll stay in pristine condition. But that's not how this game works. Our vessels, just like us, need the trials and tribulations of the rolling sea. They need to feel its waves crashing against their sides, testing their strength and resolve. Otherwise, they slowly decay while chained up in the marina.

In our lives, staying at the docks can take the shape of thinking, "That experience was so humiliating that I never want to put myself out there again." And while this, too, is a reasonable way of looking at trauma or disappointment, we must remember that, in the long term, such a mindset only gets us burned. When we don't voluntarily subject ourselves to discomfort, especially the kind that could help us move forward in life, we invite depression back into our hearts and minds. As such, we'd be wise to carefully embrace these sometimes-advantageous forms of distress, as frightening as that proposition may sound.

In practice, cautiously exploring the pain of trauma can take many forms, all of which will vary based on our desires and personal histories. For example, if we've witnessed the horrors of war or violence, *leaning in* could mean working closely with grief counselors and psychotherapists to unpack our hurts in a slow, careful way. Over time, these trained professionals will help us move through the atrocities we've encountered and show us it's okay to talk about them.[94]

BURIED TREASURE

Those who've endured such despair know the potential gold here is simply getting back to normal functioning and experiencing life once more. When caught in the throes of PTSD, such regular, healthy living is almost impossible. Until we learn to move through or make sense of what we've experienced, we'll find it very difficult to open our treasure chest. Though it will likely take time and a lot of pain, with the help of our doctors, we'll eventually crack the lock on that safe.

As another example, let's say our classmates mocked us throughout grade school for the outlandish paintings we used to produce. So much so, in fact, that we learned to associate our art with ridicule and, in turn, gave up our creative and passionate endeavors altogether. While this may seem like a trivial thing to some, I can assure you that's anything but the case. To say we should simply grab our brushes and start painting again would mean to overlook the potential severity of the trauma. In reality, that pain isn't just likely to make us not want to grab our art supplies — it might also take such a task off our radar altogether.

To up the ante here, let's also pretend we now find ourselves in the grips of a professional career detached from any real meaning or excitement. This detachment leaves us dissatisfied with our pursuits and somewhat disillusioned by life in general. While I don't want to romanticize such a situation or its potential solution too much, I do think it's important to take a step back here and try to reconnect with ourselves and the dreams in our hearts. In doing so, it's possible we re-spark our energies and break free from our career-driven malaise.

Sometimes we can do that on our own, and other times, we'll need the assistance of a professional. Thanks to our traumas and repression, we may have trouble remembering what those dreams were or why we abandoned them in the first place. That's one reason working with a therapist can be so valuable — such folks can help us rediscover our lost aims, cautiously remove the pain associated with them, and put them back on our maps.

Now, of course, I can't guarantee any one specific strategy will work for any one particular person. Still, given what we've talked about here, I'd feel confident that some soul searching in the comfort of a trained professional could at least help us realize our unhappiness is not a product of life in general — just our disconnection from it. Once we reconnect with what drives us and discover, on a deep, psychological level, that pursuing it won't lead to extreme levels of pain or danger, I think we'll find ourselves reinvigorated once more.

And while I hope these examples shed some light on what it might look like to unpack trauma and rekindle one's zest for life, I do want to mention they're not the only ones out there. I merely tell them to help you make some connections to past hurts and detachments of your own.

Though the ways those pains and disconnections could come about are virtually endless, I think hearing a few concrete examples still helps us consider our own lost treasures and see that moving toward them once again is okay. If we do that for long enough, with the assistance of the right people, we'll eventually unlock our metaphorical chests and enjoy a unique form of riches.

BATTENING DOWN THE HATCHES

Despite our leveraging of the various biological, psychological, and social remedies we've covered, the gyre may still emerge at some point on our oceanic journeys. Such is life. But that doesn't mean things are hopeless for us or that we should simply sit around and accept our despair. Instead, it signifies that we sometimes need more out-of-the-box, quickly implementable strategies to help fill the gaps. These strategies are how we metaphorically batten down the hatches and give ourselves a better chance of weathering the storm.

The first of those tactics is a relatively simple one — exercise. Now, before we dive into it, I need to mention two quick things. First, even if you're limited in your physical abilities, you can still benefit from the concepts in this section by assuming the word *exercise* refers to any type of physical stress that helps take your mind off your troubles. If traditional forms aren't feasible, that's okay. Simply concentrate on whichever ones work for you, use the sauna to get your heart rate up, or find a quiet place to meditate.

Second, I don't exactly expect this high-level strategy to blow your socks off. After all, when we're depressed, some of the last things we feel like doing are pulling ourselves out of bed, getting off the couch, or heading outdoors; our pain weighs us down and saps us of the necessary vigor. In these moments of despair, many of us know we could boost our mood by engaging in such activities. The problem is, we just don't have the energy.

Yet, sometimes our melancholic frames of mind also blind us to these notions, and that kind of shortsightedness can be challenging to overcome. Nevertheless, the more reasons and reminders we have for embracing physical stress at our disposal, the more likely we'll be to look past our pain and seek exertion. That's why I want to cover two more of them here.

The first is anecdotal but intriguing all the same, and it stems back to the etymology of one of the most important words associated with depression: emotion. When we look at the foundations of this word, we find it comes from the Latin term "emovere," which means to "move out" or "move through." Thus, to create some more positive emotions in our lives, it seems we need to leave a particular location or proceed through something. Our houses and our pain, respectively, would be good places to start.

The second reminder is a bit more scientific, and it comes from a 1999 study conducted by researchers at Duke University.[95] This particular study tells us exercise can be just as effective as antidepressant drugs in treating our misery.

In it, Dr. James Blumenthal and colleagues assigned participants to one of three groups: one adhering to an antidepressant medication regimen, another adhering to an aerobic exercise plan, and a final one adhering to both. In the two exercise-related cohorts, subjects took part in prescheduled fitness classes three times a week, at seventy to eighty-five percent of their maximum heart rates. At the end of the sixteen-week study, Blumenthal and his team found that all three groups exhibited statistically significant reductions in depressive symptoms, as measured in part by Aaron Beck's Depression Inventory.

After drawing that conclusion, however, the team decided it needed a placebo group, as it would be the only way to ensure the treatments administered in the trial were as effective as presumed. With that efficacy in mind, it conducted the study again, though this time, in an expanded fashion.

In that subsequent rendition, all three original cohorts exhibited statistically significant decreases in depressive symptoms once more, while participants in the new placebo group remained just as melancholic as they'd been for quite some time. That meant the medication and exercise plans were indeed working as suspected.

In addition, the team now had enough evidence to show that those who exercised regularly in the months following the original version of the study were fifty percent less likely to relapse into despair than those who did not. For Blumenthal's crew, that finding was a proverbial cherry on top — one that solidified the idea that physical exertion is effective in the face of depression.

Yet, as much as that conclusion helps us in the mental health realm, it still leaves us wondering: Just *why* is it true? Since I'm not a biologist or neuroscientist, I won't pretend to know all the intricacies of the complex answers to that question. However, I think a simple explanation is that exercise forces us to get out of our heads and back into our bodies, which temporarily rids us of the unwanted emotions emanating from such treacherous places.

Another reason exercise is so effective in the battle against despair is it blends seamlessly with many of our other *feel-good* strategies; when we couple it with these additional tactics, we extract even more benefit from it. As an example of this sort of thing, we can combine physical activity with mood-boosting social connection by hitting the gym with a friend, playing pickup basketball with our coworkers, or attending a group rowing class.

Or, if we're not feeling particularly outgoing, we can instead use our *solo* exercise time to get ourselves pumped up or inspired. The best way to do this is by working out with headphones and listening to our favorite, up-tempo songs. With the help of such tunes and our physical movements, we inject energy and spirit back into our bodies — two things we're often missing when caught in the throes of the vortex.

One last reason exercise is so helpful is that it offers us a reliable way to fill our calendars with exciting and presence-inducing experiences. These events are so critical because, when it comes to depression, we often find we have nothing to look forward to — and that only exacerbates our negative emotions. However, when we sign up for our favorite workouts or simply plan a hike, we mitigate that future-looking problem by giving ourselves reasons to get out of bed and keep going each day.

Regardless of how we choose to incorporate these exertion-based insights into our lives, we must remember to do so regularly by getting and staying active. To give a specific recommendation, I'd say you should aim to work out for about thirty minutes, three to six times a week, depending on the activity itself and what feels suitable to you and your schedule. Limit yourself to fifteen minutes if you're using the sauna, however, and don't be afraid to go slow if you're just getting started. There's no need to overdo it early on and hurt yourself.

While we're on the subject of things we can do in the biological realm of our biopsychosocial model to help with depression, I want to quickly cover another strategy. This one isn't for the faint of heart, however: taking a cold shower daily. Now, as crazy as that idea may sound, there's actually some science to back up its effectiveness in treating the affliction.

According to that science, our modern lives lack many of the stressors our ancestors once experienced through their daily routines. Some of those stressors included running from predators and hunting fish on frosty swims. Such inconveniences, much like most of the discomforts we voluntarily lean into nowadays, kept our forebears out of harm's way.

Today, when we take a cold shower, we emulate those ancestral, frosty swims and expose ourselves to an acute form of beneficial pain. That discomfort changes our body temperatures, stimulates our sympathetic nervous systems, and activates cold receptors on our skin. Those receptors then send electrical impulses to our brains and produce a somewhat antidepressant-like effect.[96]

Though the related research is still in its infancy, studies featuring small numbers of participants have shown that this remedy can work quite well. Yet, what makes this tactic even more interesting is that we can easily combine it with the previous one we discussed; we can end our workouts with cold showers, giving ourselves a double dose of depression-fighting help.

Now, before we wrap up this section, there's one final, biology-based strategy I want to put forth, and it's to supplement our diets with omega-3 fatty acids, such as those derived from fish oil. Unlike exercise and cold showers, however, this one isn't an in-the-moment way of boosting our happiness levels. That said, I'd be remiss if I didn't discuss it.

What the research on these supplements suggests is that the polyunsaturated fatty acids they contain can be beneficial in treating depression.[97] Though there are many convoluted factors behind this conclusion, the three main ones are: the anti-inflammatory effects omega-3 fatty acids provide, the direct modifications such acids make to our cells, and the modifications they coordinate via protein signaling.

Of course, that's complicated stuff. But let's focus on the bottom line here and what the science indicates — a regimen of omega-3s can help treat despair. And while I'm not a doctor or nutritionist and, therefore, can't and won't tell you to start that regimen, I invite you to talk about it with your physician and read the literature I've referenced and noted above. These supplements are relatively inexpensive, and there are vegan varieties available as well, though those versions tend to be a bit pricier.

SOMETIMES WE DO HAVE TO FIGHT

In the first book of this series, I talked extensively about how grappling with anxiety is a loser's game. When we push back on our bodies' fight-flight-or-freeze responses, we simply make them worse. After all, tension plus tension equals, well, more tension, so what we often view as a winning formula is, in reality, one that sends us further into overdrive.

When it comes to depression, however, this same kind of argument *doesn't* hold. There's a simple reason for this, and it's that, even though anxiety and depression are related and often comorbid diseases,[98] the internal states they bring about are almost direct opposites of one another. With anxiety, we encounter something that resembles hyperactivity, whereas, with depression, we experience sluggishness and apathy. Though it can be undeniably challenging to rally against that sluggishness at the height of our misery, we not only *can* do such a thing — we also *should*. For, if we don't, we risk getting pulled into the abyss for excruciatingly long periods.

Yet, one of the reasons we often overlook such a tactic is that we sometimes arrive at depression *from* anxiety. That is, even after we've learned to manage the latter in a calm and collected fashion, we still occasionally slip into the former on the other side of the metaphorical Strait of Messina. As a result, we often take our non-fighting approach with us into the maelstrom. And that's not only incredibly unhelpful but also profoundly confusing. Here's why.

BATTENING DOWN THE HATCHES

When we tell ourselves we can't or shouldn't battle our despair, we lose our last line of defense against it. Since one of the definitions of depression is a "pushing down," when we abandon our will to fight, we allow its dark forces to drive us into the depths of the sea. Thus, if we don't want to drown or shipwreck, we're going to have to muster up that will again; yes, sometimes, we *do* have to fight.

When I talk to people about their depression, some of them mirror this sentiment by saying they're in a fight for their lives. Though not a literal battle, I don't think we can overstate the accuracy of such a metaphor. These folks are pushing back against helplessness, hopelessness, and gloom. They're reaching out, finding support, and continuing on, even when things look bleak.

While we can never know for sure who will make it through and who won't, it's not always these people that concern me the most. No, the folks that I think are more at risk of depression devastation are those who have no fight left at all. Don't get me wrong — I'm not casting judgment on such people. I realize how onerous depression is, and I empathize with these sufferers wholeheartedly. I'm just saying that not having any fight left in us sounds a lot like giving up, and we all know the horrific consequences associated with that course of action.

WHO OR WHAT WILL YOU FIGHT FOR?

Of course, to keep going, we must have a reason or purpose. Lacking either, in fact, is one of the most common and trying sources of isolation-related depression. Folks who are both distraught and cut off from society and their social circles sometimes feel so disconnected that they see no point in persisting.

This is the precise reason we need people and causes for which we'll fight. They're the Nietzsche-approved ideas and folks that float alongside us and help us adjust our sails quickly. When we're stuck in our heads and blinded by hopelessness, we often can't see these sources of strength, even if they indeed exist. That's why it's essential to come up with a list of them and keep it somewhere we'll remember. Something like a digital note on our cell phones would do the trick.

When we revisit such lists, we realize we actually do have things and people for whom we can and will persevere. For me, these people are my late grandparents, grandfather, parents, brother, sister-in-law, nephew, and niece. These are the same sorts of people with whom we should feel comfortable discussing our struggles. They're our loved ones, after all, and they've been through pain as well. They'll understand our plight, listen, and support us.

Now, this is going to be a bit unsettling, but I have to say it. If you ever find yourself driven to the brink of self-harm, call the National Suicide Prevention Hotline (1-800-273-8255) and return to your list. Think about your loved ones. Those people would be devastated if you weren't here anymore. I don't mean that halfheartedly, so I'll say it again. If you left this earth, yes, they'd understand the pain you were in, but they'd also be completely and utterly heartbroken. And, to tell you the truth, I'd be, too.

Though I realize how heavy those words are, I was serious when I said this would be unnerving. Despite that heaviness, there's a method to my madness here. No, I'm trying to guilt you. I just want to reconnect you to your driving forces and remind you of one of your strongest defenses against the leviathan. If my words struck a chord, it shows you still have some fight left in you. That's a good thing. Harness that fight, strengthen it, and give it all you have. This could very well be the battle of a lifetime.

PROVING DEPRESSION WRONG

At the core of depression are several lies about our lives, ourselves, and the world. These lies are the ones our despondency tries to convince us of as it pulls us down into its endless vortex. These false notions include the idea that we'll never get to wherever it is we're aiming and that we shouldn't even try to — or the harrowing belief that our lives are meaningless and always will be.

As much as depression tries to persuade us of these ideas, and as much as we buy into them at times, they simply aren't accurate. Specifically, it's up to us where we're heading on our journeys, whether or not we're going to get there, and how we'll create and find meaning along the way. Typically, the emergence of such lies simply indicates we're disconnected from our sources of that meaning and in constant, soul-crushing pain. Of course, it's hard to see past them amid our agony, but that doesn't make them true.

After we battle these lies for long enough during our melancholy-filled episodes, we come to a fork in the road. That fork is where we have to decide between giving in to the pain and doubling down on our fight. To choose the latter — the path I recommend — we'll inevitably need to set a chip on our shoulders and tell depression we aren't messing around anymore. That chip pushes us to put this foe in its place and prove that it, and all the terrifying notions with which it arrives, are entirely false.

In practice, this takes the shape of adopting an "I'll show you" attitude. It means turning depression into an enemy and fighting it wherever in the ocean it cares to lead us or reconnecting with life in such a way that we start getting to where we want to go. It means developing enough purpose through our relationships and daily activities to unmask our melancholy and reveal it as the phony that it truly is.

In my opinion, this approach works because depression is a disease often marked by excess rationality, a condition in which we press so far into our logic-based minds that we convince ourselves of even the darkest and most daunting possibilities. To escape such fears, we need the *opposite* of logic: a dose of *irrationality*. We need faith in a compelling future and our ability to enact change in our lives — and that's what this strategy provides us.

BATTENING DOWN THE HATCHES

At the heart of this "I'll prove you wrong" approach is the challenge to make something of ourselves and develop meaning. The best and most relevant part of it is that it's not rational. When we're forcefully called to action, when we truly have our backs against the wall, the facts surrounding our circumstances don't matter nearly as much. All that matters are results, and when we're under the influence of such empowering challenges, we'll do whatever it takes to create them.

Upon accepting these calls to action, we also adopt new mindsets. As a result, our outlooks often change. For example, if we've lost hope on our journeys toward personal achievement, these mindsets can push us to say to our depression, "Oh, you don't think I'm capable of holding down a job and having coworkers who care about me? Well, then, I'll fight with every fiber in my being to make it happen anyway. Watch me." Or, on the quest for meaning in our lives, these same mindsets push us to say to our foe, "Oh, you're here to tell me life is meaningless? Well, it's now my mission to prove the complete opposite. Watch me fill this journey with more of it than you ever could've fathomed."

Of course, we all have our ways of dealing with difficulty, so it might not seem natural to put such a chip on our shoulders. Even though that may be the case, I still think doing so gives us one of the best means of escaping the abyss because it reinvigorates our fight and provides us the strength and determination to keep moving.

But that's not to say we can fight forever, nor that we should. There's a reason for this: waging war takes effort. And lots of it. As such, we must know when to engage and when to put the cannons away. Otherwise, we may find ourselves brawling even when we no longer need to and, in turn, subjecting ourselves to another source of burnout that could ultimately cause our melancholy to arise once more.

Thus, the most efficient game plan would be to fight depression just long enough to force it into a manageable container. Once we've done that, we'll take that container, dig a hole at the shore, bury it deep underground, and cover it in our ship's refuse. That's right. A foe like that doesn't even deserve sand for a home. No, that would be too good for it.

Rather than bury our *trauma* or the parts of ourselves we need in order to thrive, we'll bury *our despair* at the beach. We'll put it in its place and get back on with our lives. And, if it ever does escape its receptacle, we'll return and fight it again.

CONTINUING ON THROUGH DEPRESSION

While I think the concept of fighting is a beneficial and necessary one on this arduous journey, I discuss it not to make light of our struggles or suggest that getting past them is always so straightforward. This is depression, after all — one of the most trying conflicts we'll ever encounter. Instead, I merely elaborate on it to equip us with a new strategy and give us another lifeline we can leverage when we find ourselves in the depths of the chasm.

BATTENING DOWN THE HATCHES

I'm also aware that pushing back against our despair won't seem like a feasible or useful idea all the time. Without a doubt, there will be days when such an approach looks a lot more like self-help nonsense. After all, depression is often so overwhelming it neutralizes most, if not all, of our efforts. As such, it may also counteract this tactic's expected helpfulness — and that's quite understandable.

Yet, even when we find this to be the case, we must proceed in some capacity. If not for ourselves, then for our loved ones, our future selves, or those we'll eventually impact. We must engage in empowering activities that distract us from our anguish. We must put our heads down and continue on because, sometimes, the only thing that keeps us going is the fact that we keep going at all.

If we just continue plowing ahead, things will inevitably get better. Given the state we're in, we might not be able to see that right now, but it's the truth nonetheless. Okay, maybe not the *party until dawn* kind of better, but still, undeniably and unequivocally so.

This lessening of our despair, and these moments of relief, are what we should set our sights on, for they absolutely will come if we just keep moving. Yes, there will be days when all seems lost. There will be times when we have less than no hope. I cannot overstate such a reality. However, go on we must, for it's the only viable option.

As civil rights activist James Baldwin wrote in his 1963 book entitled *The Fire Next Time*, when we're continually surviving the worst that life can throw our way, we'll eventually stop fearing what it can bring us. We'll have been through it all already, and we'll know what to expect.[99] Thus, whether we're in the middle of despair right now or anxiously waiting for it to emerge once more, we should continue on. We should batten down the hatches, knowing our ships will soon be so resilient we might not even need to anymore.

A MARINER'S SALUTE

Throughout our time together, we've discussed the various ways depression can emerge in our lives. We've seen the impact our internal states have on our mental health and how the abyss can reappear when we're not in the right frame of mind. Additionally, we've witnessed how our environments influence those states and, sometimes, sequentially plunge us into anxiety and depression.

We've also discovered the exact ways by which the abyss works. We've looked into its heart and realized how, when we're not present or healthfully distracted by passion-filled and meaningful pursuits, we invite this monstrosity toward our boats yet again. Moreover, we've come to know the insidiousness of such a structure by seeing its wormhole reopen and try to lure us back in.

We've also explored the less obvious aspects of depression. We've concluded that some kind of suffering — despair being one of them — is inevitable in our lives. If we want to avoid the more agonizing types, we must regularly seek uplifting forms of discomfort, such as learning new skills or temporarily giving up our favorite junk foods.

Another one of those less apparent parts we've addressed is the importance of maintaining balance in our lives. When our biological, psychological, and social spheres fall out of equilibrium with one another, our risk of encountering the maelstrom increases. In the same vein, we've concluded how important our values are in finding such balance; when we prioritize and pursue the wrong aims, we can capsize or become depressed without even realizing why.

We've also covered the important subject of trauma — our past experiences of shock or distress — and how it can hinder us from living out our values. Luckily, we've learned the power of being courageous and vulnerable despite the pains associated with such experiences as well. When we're willing to unpack them in the safety of professionals, we give ourselves a decent chance of reconnecting with our lost hopes and dreams and digging up some figurative pirate booty.

Lastly, we've rediscovered the importance of continuing to fight through depression. We've seen just how critical it is to have a list of people and causes we care about, for they're what keep us going in the face of despair. These are the same things for which we'd persist regardless of the circumstances.

Now that we've covered all the core, abyss-related material and are preparing to part ways, I want to give you some final words of wisdom before you continue on your journey. The first is that while I can never know all the pain you've been through, I do know you're strong beyond measure.

Depression can be so darn hard to deal with. The forces that lead to it can, too. Despite that difficulty and the war of emotions that's come alongside it, you're still here, pushing forward. Hats off to you, mate. I respect the heck out of you for it.

The second thing I want to tell you is it's clear you're a fighter. You've pushed through the darkness to improve your own life, that of someone you love, or both. Yet, regardless of why you picked this book up in the first place, you can rest assured you're now a mariner of the highest rank. That means I'd have you on my ship anytime.

The third piece of wisdom I want to leave you with is to remember to have compassion for yourself and all you go through. In our culture, we learn to be hard on ourselves and not settle for anything less than greatness. While there's nothing wrong with aiming high in life, beating ourselves up rarely helps us achieve such aims. In fact, it usually only stifles us and makes us feel worse. Since winning the battle against despair requires keeping ourselves in empowering and uplifting states, I think we're better off ditching self-criticism altogether.

If you ever feel you actually *should* be hard on yourself, remember just how severe and formidable a disease depression is. There's nothing — and I mean nothing — to be ashamed of in dealing with it. Instead of berating yourself over it, try approaching your tribulations with more understanding. Talk to yourself as if you were your own best friend. You know, the kind who tells you exactly what you need to hear but also isn't afraid to come over uninvited and deliver a big hug, either.

In reality, so many folks across the globe struggle with depression. We most certainly aren't the only ones, nor are we the only people who struggle in general. Whether we realize it or not, almost everyone we know is fighting a battle we can't see. It could be self-consciousness, anxiety, addiction, or something entirely different, but trust me, it's there, below the surface. The next time you notice you're being hard on yourself due to your depression, think of these other struggling folks and remember you're not alone.

Of course, if we wanted to, we could let that same lesson be the very thing that sends us into the wormhole to the abyss. After all, if everyone struggles, how can we ever escape pain and find fulfillment? Though it would seem like a legitimate question, it misses two key points of the struggle process. The first is that while suffering is inevitable, it's not constant or permanent. Just like depression itself, all our tribulations eventually subside and allow us to catch our breath. Oddly enough, it's this pushing and pulling between struggle and rest that often leads us to the happiness we thought such pain was trying to keep us from in the first place.

The second thing such pessimistic thinking overlooks is that suffering, though it may sound it, isn't necessarily a bad word; there are both good *and* bad forms. Some positive ones include tough training sessions, long work hours in pursuit of our dreams, and late nights spent tutoring our children. All of them help us better enjoy the eventual downtime we unlock, as well as any potential fruits of our labor, once we finally get through them.

When we stop and think about these pursuits at a high level, we see that almost any form of striving, be it trying to get into our dream college or saving for a down payment on a house, is just another flavor of struggle in our lives. The thing about these specific types, however, is that they're the good and necessary kinds. The kinds that put energy in our tanks and allow us to come alive. When we connect with these beneficial forms, as well as the wisdom they provide, we help ourselves avoid any abyss-related wormholes that the subject of suffering sometimes reveals.

So, with all that said, we now arrive at the final words of this book — the last oceanic insight I have to give you. Falling in line with what we just discussed, and as you've probably heard throughout your years, life is a journey, not a destination. Though we often think everything will be fantastic for the rest of our days if we just make it to the paradise islands on our maps, that's not how life works.

As frustrating as it may be to hear, our satisfaction on those islands will eventually wane if we stay too long. Though we should always celebrate when we reach such destinations and take the time to disembark, explore, and enjoy all they have to offer, we should also remember there's yet another voyage ahead. We should look forward to that voyage and relish it when it arrives. For, in life, we can never stop sailing. Otherwise, the chasm comes calling for us.

No matter where your maritime adventures may take you, remember, that dreaded whirlpool can emerge when you least expect it. At this very instant, it may be countless leagues away or right in front of your eyes. Wherever it is, know this: If you apply everything we've talked about and sail into the wind with all your might, you can evade that gyre for longer periods and maintain the momentum required for escaping it when it does appear. For, as we've seen, though downright brutal at times, depression is beatable. Never forget that. It may take everything you've got in your arsenal, but luckily, that's now a whole lot. Give it hell, sailor.

ACKNOWLEDGEMENTS

When I set out to write this book, I posted online and asked those in my network if they'd had any previous experience with depression. Being the sensitive topic that it is, I only expected a few responses. To my surprise, about twenty people wrote back and graciously offered their time and perspectives.

I chatted with as many of those folks as our schedules allowed and used their stories to help guide the research and content in the pages you just finished reading. Their personal accounts allowed me to better understand the disease as a whole and approach it from multiple angles. Without the input of these friends, this book wouldn't be what it is today.

For their courage, insights, and support, I'd like to thank all my interviewees: Aaron, Bryce, Camille, Carson, Christine, Dan, Danny, Grace, Jessie, John, Justine, Liz, Mark, Miguel, Paul, Peter, Richie, and Walter. I hope I did your stories justice, even if I didn't explicitly tell them in the manuscript. Thanks for sitting down with me and opening up. It meant a lot.

To my designers, Akhil and Ted, thank you so much for your contributions. I really believe that the cover of this book and the look and feel of the "Get Out of Your Head" brand, as a whole, portray the collective struggle of me and my audience. I know both sets of designs resonate strongly with countless

ACKNOWLEDGEMENTS

readers, so thanks for creating two visual identities we can all relate to and rally around.

To my editor, Angi, thank you for continuing to provide your wisdom and prowess. When I'm too close to the manuscript, it's difficult for me to see all the same things you can. Thanks for coming in and offering that compassionate and understanding view that helps me connect with and appeal to more people.

To my readers and supporters of the blog and first book, thank you for your messages, encouragement, and enthusiasm. It was an honor to hear from many of you and learn how your interactions with the GOOYH brand influenced your lives in various ways. I admire your bravery and perseverance so much. You are all warriors. Keep fighting.

To Mom and Dad, thanks for always being there to chat, offer support, or just hang out. I'm so lucky to have you both.

And, lastly, to my late grandmother, Nana. There's not a day that goes by where I don't think of and miss you dearly. Thanks for all the life lessons and wonderful memories.

I NEED YOUR HELP

Thanks so much for purchasing and reading *Get Out of Your Head Volume 2: Navigating the Abyss of Depression*. I hope you enjoyed it.

Before you go, I have one small favor to ask. Would you mind heading to Amazon and writing a review for this book? I'm on a mission to help anyone I can with their mental health struggles, and every review this book receives helps it climb Amazon's rankings and reach new readers. With enough reviews, we can impact countless people.

I read all my reviews and take them very seriously. I also use them to make updates to my books and get ideas for future projects. Every little bit helps.

Or, if you're feeling extra daring, head to www.getoutofyourhead.com/merch and grab some brand swag to show off on social media using #getoutofyourheadbook.

Thanks,

Brian

ABOUT THE AUTHOR

Brian Sachetta is a software developer, blogger, and mental health advocate. He resides in Boston, where he is happily surrounded by friends and family. If you'd like to get in touch with him, please send him an email at the address below:

brian@getoutofyourhead.com

NOTES / SOURCES

[1] Hasin, Deborah S, et al. "Epidemiology of Adult DSM-5 Major Depressive Disorder and Its Specifiers in the United States." *JAMA Psychiatry*, vol. 75, no. 4, 2018, pp. 336–346., https://doi.org/10.1001/jamapsychiatry.2017.4602.

[2] "Facts & Statistics: Anxiety and Depression Association of America, ADAA." Facts & Statistics | *Anxiety and Depression Association of America, ADAA*, https://adaa.org/understanding-anxiety/facts-statistics.

[3] Greenberg, Paul E., et al. "The Economic Burden of Adults with Major Depressive Disorder in the United States (2005 and 2010)." *The Journal of Clinical Psychiatry*, vol. 76, no. 02, 2015, pp. 155–162., https://doi.org/10.4088/jcp.14m09298.

[4] Ledford, Heidi. "Medical Research: If Depression Were Cancer." *Nature*, vol. 515, no. 7526, 2014, pp. 182–184., https://doi.org/10.1038/515182a.

[5] "NCHS Dataline." *Public Health Reports* vol. 127,2 (2012): 228–229.

[6] Pratt, Laura A, et al. "Antidepressant Use Among Persons Aged 12 and Over: United States, 2011–2014." *Centers for Disease*

Control and Prevention, CDC, Aug. 2017,
https://www.cdc.gov/nchs/data/databriefs/db283.pdf.

[7] Weinberger, A. H., et al. "Trends in Depression Prevalence in the USA from 2005 to 2015: Widening Disparities in Vulnerable Groups." *Psychological Medicine*, vol. 48, no. 8, 2018, pp. 1308–1315., doi:10.1017/S0033291717002781.

[8] Engel, George L. "The Need for a New Medical Model: A Challenge for Biomedicine." *Science*, vol. 196, no. 4286, 1977, pp. 129–136., https://doi.org/10.1126/science.847460.

[9] Molendijk, Marc, et al. "Diet Quality and Depression Risk: A Systematic Review and Dose-Response Meta-Analysis of Prospective Studies." *Journal of Affective Disorders*, vol. 226, 2018, pp. 346–354., https://doi.org/10.1016/j.jad.2017.09.022.

[10] Walden University. "Power Posing: What Every Mental Health Professional Should Know." Walden University, *Walden University*, 25 Mar. 2021, https://www.waldenu.edu/online-masters-programs/ms-in-clinical-mental-health-counseling/resource/power-posing-what-every-mental-health-professional-should-know.

[11] Harris, Karen, et al. Bain & Company, 2018, pp. 18–30, *Labor 2030: The Collision of Demographics, Automation and Inequality.*

---

[12] "World 'Nearing Critical Point of No Return' on Climate Change, Delegate Warns, as Second Committee Debates Sustainable Development." *United Nations*, United Nations, 15 Oct. 2018, https://www.un.org/press/en/2018/gaef3500.doc.htm.

[13] Nietzsche, Friedrich W. "Aphorism 146." *Beyond Good and Evil: Prelude to a Philosophy of the Future*, Penguin Books, 1990.

[14] "The Fraternal Twins of Mood Disorders." Aurora Behavioral Health, https://www.auroraarizona.com/sites/default/files/attachments/depression%20and%20anxiety%20-%20the%20fraternal%20twins%20of%20mood%20disorders.pdf.

[15] Hedegaard, Holly, et al. "Increase in Suicide Mortality in the United States, 1999-2018." National Center for Health Statistics, Apr. 2020.

[16] Xu, Jiaquan, et al. "Mortality in the United States, 2015." National Center for Health Statistics, Dec. 2016.

[17] "Fourth National Climate Assessment, Volume II: Impacts, Risks, and Adaptation in the United States." *NCA4*, Oct. 2018, https://nca2018.globalchange.gov/.

[18] *Diagnostic and Statistical Manual of Mental Disorders: DSM-5*, 5th ed., CBS Publishers & Distributors, Pvt. Ltd., New Delhi, 2017, p. 160–161.

[19] Klein, Daniel N. "Classification of Depressive Disorders in the DSM-V: Proposal for a Two-Dimension System." *Journal of Abnormal Psychology*, vol. 117, no. 3, 2008, pp. 552–560., https://doi.org/10.1037/0021-843x.117.3.552.

[20] *Diagnostic and Statistical Manual of Mental Disorders: DSM-5*, 5th ed., CBS Publishers & Distributors, Pvt. Ltd., New Delhi, 2017, pp. 160–161.

[21] Seligman, Martin E. "Learned Helplessness." *Annual Review of Medicine*, vol. 23, no. 1, 1972, pp. 407–412., https://doi.org/10.1146/annurev.me.23.020172.002203.

[22] Maier, Steven F., and Linda R. Watkins. "Stressor Controllability and Learned Helplessness: The Roles of the Dorsal Raphe Nucleus, Serotonin, and Corticotropin-Releasing Factor." *Neuroscience & Biobehavioral Reviews*, vol. 29, no. 4-5, 2005, pp. 829–841., https://doi.org/10.1016/j.neubiorev.2005.03.021.

[23] Weiss, Jay M., et al. "Behavioral Depression Produced by an Uncontrollable Stressor: Relationship to Norepinephrine, Dopamine, and Serotonin Levels in Various Regions of Rat Brain." *Brain Research Reviews*, vol. 3, no. 2, 1981, pp. 167–205., https://doi.org/10.1016/0165-0173(81)90005-9.

[24] *Diagnostic and Statistical Manual of Mental Disorders: DSM-5*, 5th ed., CBS Publishers & Distributors, Pvt. Ltd., New Delhi, 2017, p. 155.

[25] *Diagnostic and Statistical Manual of Mental Disorders: DSM-5*, 5th ed., CBS Publishers & Distributors, Pvt. Ltd., New Delhi, 2017, p. 187.

[26] Sansone, Randy A, and Lori A Sansone. "Dysthymic Disorder: Forlorn and Overlooked?" *Psychiatry*, Matrix Medical Communications, May 2009, https://www.ncbi.nlm.nih.gov/pmc/articles/PMC2719439/.

[27] Kent, Allen, and James G Williams. "Finite-State Machines." *Encyclopedia of Computer Science and Technology*, vol. 25, CRC Press, 1991, pp. 73–78.

[28] Maslow, Abraham H. *The Psychology of Science*, Harper & Row, 1966, p. 15.

[29] Nisbett, Richard E., and David E. Kanouse. "Obesity, Food Deprivation, and Supermarket Shopping Behavior." *Journal of Personality and Social Psychology*, vol. 12, no. 4, 1969, pp. 289–294., https://doi.org/10.1037/h0027799.

[30] Schwarz, Norbert, and Gerald L. Clore. "Mood, Misattribution, and Judgments of Well-Being: Informative and Directive Functions of Affective States." *Journal of Personality and*

Social Psychology, vol. 45, no. 3, 1983, pp. 513–523., https://doi.org/10.1037/0022-3514.45.3.513.

[31] MacLeod, Andrew K., and Angela Byrne. "Anxiety, Depression, and the Anticipation of Future Positive and Negative Experiences." *Journal of Abnormal Psychology*, vol. 105, no. 2, 1996, pp. 286–289., https://doi.org/10.1037/0021-843x.105.2.286.

[32] Gentry, Arvel. "A Review of Modern Sail Theory." Boeing Commercial Airplane Company, 12 Sept. 1981.

[33] Beck, Judith S., and Aaron T. Beck. *Cognitive Behavior Therapy: Basics and Beyond*, 2nd ed., The Guilford Press, New York, NY, 2011, pp. 19–20.

[34] Beck, Aaron T. "The Past and Future of Cognitive Therapy." *The Journal of Psychotherapy Practice and Research*, vol. 6, no. 4, 1997, pp. 276–284.

[35] Beck, Aaron T. "An Inventory for Measuring Depression." *Archives of General Psychiatry*, vol. 4, no. 6, 1961, p. 561., https://doi.org/10.1001/archpsyc.1961.01710120031004.

[36] "Beck Depression Inventory (BDI)." *Addiction Research Center*, https://arc.psych.wisc.edu/self-report/beck-depression-inventory-bdi/.

[37] Wang, L., et al. "Cognitive Trio: Relationship with Major Depression and Clinical Predictors in Han Chinese Women." *Psychological Medicine*, vol. 43, no. 11, 2013, pp. 2265–2275., https://doi.org/10.1017/s0033291713000160.

[38] Gorman, Jack M, and Jeremy D Coplan. "Comorbid Depression and Anxiety Spectrum Disorders." *Depression and Anxiety*, vol. 57, no. 4, Jan. 1996, pp. 34–41.

[39] Frisbee, Jefferson C., et al. "An Unpredictable Chronic Mild Stress Protocol for Instigating Depressive Symptoms, Behavioral Changes and Negative Health Outcomes in Rodents." *Journal of Visualized Experiments*, no. 106, 2015, https://doi.org/10.3791/53109.

[40] Maier, Steven F., and Linda R. Watkins. "Stressor Controllability, Anxiety, and Serotonin." *Cognitive Therapy and Research*, vol. 22, no. 6, 1998, pp. 595–613., https://doi.org/10.1023/a:1018794104325.

[41] Brown, George W, and Tirril Harris. *Social Origins of Depression*, Reprint ed., Psychology Press, 2001, pp. 3–116.

[42] Keynes, John Maynard. "Economic Possibilities for Our Grandchildren." *Yale University Department of Economics*, 1930, http://www.econ.yale.edu/smith/econ116a/keynes1.pdf.

[43] Price, John S. "Evolutionary Aspects of Anxiety Disorders." *Dialogues in Clinical Neuroscience*, vol. 5, no. 3, 2003, pp. 223–236., https://doi.org/10.31887/dcns.2003.5.3/jprice.

[44] Leary, Mark R. "Emotional Responses to Interpersonal Rejection." *Emotions*, vol. 17, no. 4, 2015, pp. 435–441., https://doi.org/10.31887/dcns.2015.17.4/mleary.

[45] Neubauer, Simon, et al. "The Evolution of Modern Human Brain Shape." *Science Advances*, vol. 4, no. 1, 2018, https://doi.org/10.1126/sciadv.aao5961.

[46] Hidaka, Brandon H. "Depression As a Disease of Modernity: Explanations for Increasing Prevalence." *Journal of Affective Disorders*, vol. 140, no. 3, 2012, pp. 205–214., https://doi.org/10.1016/j.jad.2011.12.036.

[47] Hostetter, Abraham M, and Janice A Egeland. "Amish Study, I: Affective Disorders among the Amish, 1976-1980." *American Journal of Psychiatry*, vol. 140, no. 1, 1983, pp. 56–61., https://doi.org/10.1176/ajp.140.1.56.

[48] "NIMH Mental Illness." *National Institute of Mental Health*, U.S. Department of Health and Human Services, https://www.nimh.nih.gov/health/statistics/mental-illness.

[49] Ilardi, Steve. "The Epidemic and the Cure." *The Depression Cure: The Six-Step Program to Beat Depression without Drugs*, Da Capo Press, London, 2010, pp. 5–7.

[50] Kawai, Daisuke. "Social Media Paradox: Social Media Reduces Friends, Relationships, and Psychological Well-Being." https://doi.org/10.14836/ssi.3.1 31.

[51] Clark, Jenna L., et al. "Social Network Sites and Well-Being: The Role of Social Connection." *Current Directions in Psychological Science*, vol. 27, no. 1, 2017, pp. 32–37., https://doi.org/10.1177/0963721417730833.

[52] Shakya, Holly B., and Nicholas A. Christakis. "Association of Facebook Use with Compromised Well-Being: A Longitudinal Study." *American Journal of Epidemiology*, 2017, https://doi.org/10.1093/aje/kww189.

[53] Mushtaq, Raheel. "Relationship between Loneliness, Psychiatric Disorders and Physical Health? A Review on the Psychological Aspects of Loneliness." *Journal of Clinical and Diagnostic Research*, 2014, https://doi.org/10.7860/jcdr/2014/10077.4828.

[54] "The Lethality of Loneliness: John Cacioppo at TEDxDesMoines." 9 Sept. 2013, https://www.youtube.com/watch?v=_0hxl03JoA0. Accessed 21 Oct. 2021.

[55] Hawkley, Louise C., et al. "Loneliness in Everyday Life: Cardiovascular Activity, Psychosocial Context, and Health Behaviors." *Journal of Personality and Social Psychology*, vol. 85, no. 1, 2003, pp. 105–120., https://doi.org/10.1037/0022-3514.85.1.105.

[56] "University of Chicago Research Shows Link between Loneliness and Health." *The University of Chicago News Office*, 7 Aug. 2000, http://www-news.uchicago.edu/releases/00/000807.loneliness.shtml. Accessed 21 Oct. 2021.

[57] Doane, Leah D., and Emma K. Adam. "Loneliness and Cortisol: Momentary, Day-to-Day, and Trait Associations." *Psychoneuroendocrinology*, vol. 35, no. 3, 2010, pp. 430–441., https://doi.org/10.1016/j.psyneuen.2009.08.005.

[58] Cacioppo, John T., and William Patrick. "Variation, Regulation, and an Elastic Leash." *Loneliness: Human Nature and the Need for Social Connection*, Norton, New York, NY, 2009, pp. 31–32.

[59] Tiwari, Sarvada Chandra. "Loneliness: A Disease?" *Indian Journal of Psychiatry*, vol. 55, no. 4, 2013, p. 320., https://doi.org/10.4103/0019-5545.120536.

---

[60] Cacioppo, John T., et al. "Loneliness as a Specific Risk Factor for Depressive Symptoms: Cross-Sectional and Longitudinal Analyses." *Psychology and Aging*, vol. 21, no. 1, 2006, pp. 140–151., https://doi.org/10.1037/0882-7974.21.1.140.

[61] Brown, Stuart L., and Christopher C. Vaughan. "The Opposite of Work Is Not Play." *Play: How It Shapes the Brain, Opens the Imagination, and Invigorates the Soul*, Avery, New York, NY, 2010, p. 126.

[62] Solomon, Andrew. "Depression." *The Noonday Demon: An Atlas of Depression*, Scribner, New York, NY, 2003, pp. 36–37.

[63] Sahlgren, Gabriel H. "Work Longer, Live Healthier: The Relationship between Economic Activity, Health and Government Policy." *SSRN Electronic Journal*, May 2013, https://doi.org/10.2139/ssrn.2267408.

[64] Levine, Saul. "Man Plans, and God Laughs." *Psychology Today*, 26 Feb. 2016, https://www.psychologytoday.com/us/blog/our-emotional-footprint/201602/man-plans-and-god-laughs. Accessed 21 Oct. 2021.

[65] Schwartz, Barry. "Whose Fault Is It? Choice, Disappointment, and Depression." *The Paradox of Choice*, Harper Collins, New York, NY, 2004, pp. 206–208.

[66] Greene, Robert, and 50 Cent. "Respect the Process — Mastery." *The 50th Law*, Profile Books, London, 2013, p. 211.

[67] Van der Kolk, Bessel A. "Running For Your Life: The Anatomy of Survival." *The Body Keeps the Score: Brain, Mind, and Body in the Healing of Trauma*, Penguin Books, 2015, p. 55.

[68] Peterson, Jordan B. "The Hostile Brothers." *Maps of Meaning: The Architecture of Belief*, Routledge, London, 1999, p. 338.

[69] Styron, William. "V." *Darkness Visible: A Memoir of Madness*, Random House, New York, NY, 1999, p. 57.

[70] Tolstoy, Leo. *A Confession*. Dana Estes & Company, 1882.

[71] Taleb, Nassim Nicholas. "Prologue." *Antifragile: Things that Gain from Disorder*, Random House, New York, NY, 2016, pp. 3-4.

[72] Kendall, Graham. "Could an iPhone Fly Me to the Moon?" *The Independent*, Independent Digital News and Media, 15 July 2019, https://www.independent.co.uk/news/science/apollo-11-moon-landing-mobile-phones-smartphone-iphone-a8988351.html.

[73] Staddon, J. E., and D. T. Cerutti. "Operant Conditioning." *Annual Review of Psychology*, vol. 54, no. 1, 2003, pp. 115-144., https://doi.org/10.1146/annurev.psych.54.101601.145124.

74 "Religions - Taoism: Concepts within Taoism." *BBC*, BBC, 12 Nov. 2009,
https://www.bbc.co.uk/religion/religions/taoism/beliefs/concepts.shtml.

75 "Yin / Yang Theory." *TCM World*, Traditional Chinese Medicine World Foundation, 31 Aug. 2015,
https://www.tcmworld.org/what-is-tcm/yin-yang-theory/.

76 Peterson, Jordan B. "The Hostile Brothers." *Maps of Meaning: The Architecture of Belief*, Routledge, London, 1999, p. 339.

77 Dispenza, Joe. "The Chemistry of Survival." *Evolve Your Brain: The Science of Changing Your Mind*, Health Communications, Deerfield Beach, FL, 2009, p. 260.

78 Helliwell, John F, et al. 2018, *World Happiness Report*,
https://worldhappiness.report/ed/2018/. Accessed 21 Oct. 2021.

79 Abadi, Mark. "20 Lottery Winners Who Lost Every Penny." *Business Insider*, Business Insider, 21 Mar. 2019,
https://www.businessinsider.com/lottery-winners-lost-everything-2017-8.

80 Simmons, Russell, and Chris Morrow. "Law Number Five: Never Less Than Your Best." *Do You!: 12 Laws to Access the Power in You to Achieve Happiness and Success*, Gotham, New York, 2008, p. 119.

NOTES / SOURCES

[81] "75-Year Harvard Study: What Makes Us Happy?" *AP NEWS*, Associated Press, 21 Apr. 2019, https://apnews.com/6dab1e79c34e4514af8d184d951f5733.

[82] Saphire-Bernstein, Shimon, and Shelley E. Taylor. "Close Relationships and Happiness." *Oxford Handbooks Online*, 2013, https://doi.org/10.1093/oxfordhb/9780199557257.013.0060.

[83] Vaillant, George E, et al. "Grant Study of Adult Development, 1938-2000." *Harvard Dataverse*, 2010, https://doi.org/10.7910/DVN/48WRX9. Accessed 21 Oct. 2021.

[84] Jebb, Andrew T., et al. "Happiness, Income Satiation, and Turning Points around the World." *Nature Human Behaviour*, vol. 2, no. 1, 2018, pp. 33–38., https://doi.org/10.1038/s41562-017-0277-0.

[85] Kasser, Tim, and Richard M. Ryan. "A Dark Side of the American Dream: Correlates of Financial Success as a Central Life Aspiration." *Journal of Personality and Social Psychology*, vol. 65, no. 2, 1993, pp. 410–422., https://doi.org/10.1037/0022-3514.65.2.410.

[86] Peterson, Jordan B. "The Hostile Brothers." *Maps of Meaning: The Architecture of Belief*, Routledge, London, 1999, p. 468.

[87] Peterson, Jordan B. "The Hostile Brothers." *Maps of Meaning: The Architecture of Belief*, Routledge, London, 1999, p. 465.

[88] Williamson, Marianne. "Old Powers, New Powers." *Healing the Soul of America: Reclaiming Our Voices as Spiritual Citizens*, Simon & Schuster, New York, NY, 2000, p. 188.

[89] Eckersley, Richard, and Keith Dear. "Cultural Correlates of Youth Suicide." *Social Science & Medicine*, vol. 55, no. 11, 2002, pp. 1891–1904., https://doi.org/10.1016/s0277-9536(01)00319-7.

[90] "Trauma." *Psychology Today*, Sussex Publishers, https://www.psychologytoday.com/us/basics/trauma.

[91] Bisson, Jonathan I, et al. "Post-Traumatic Stress Disorder." *BMJ*, 2015, https://doi.org/10.1136/bmj.h6161.

[92] Blakey, Shannon M., et al. "Why Do Trauma Survivors Become Depressed? Testing the Behavioral Model of Depression in a Nationally Representative Sample." *Psychiatry Research*, vol. 272, 2019, pp. 587–594., https://doi.org/10.1016/j.psychres.2018.12.150.

[93] Kilpatrick, Dean G., et al. "National Estimates of Exposure to Traumatic Events and PTSD Prevalence Using DSM-IV and DSM-5 Criteria." *Journal of Traumatic Stress*, vol. 26, no. 5, 2013, pp. 537–547., https://doi.org/10.1002/jts.21848.

[94] Vitriol, Verónica, et al. "Depression and Psychological Trauma: An Overview Integrating Current Research and Specific Evidence of Studies in the Treatment of Depression in Public Mental Health Services in Chile." *Depression Research and Treatment*, vol. 2014, 2014, pp. 1–10., https://doi.org/10.1155/2014/608671.

[95] Blumenthal, James A., et al. "Effects of Exercise Training on Older Patients with Major Depression." *Archives of Internal Medicine*, vol. 159, no. 19, 1999, https://doi.org/10.1001/archinte.159.19.2349.

[96] Shevchuk, Nikolai A. "Adapted Cold Shower as a Potential Treatment for Depression." *Medical Hypotheses*, vol. 70, no. 5, 2008, pp. 995–1001., https://doi.org/10.1016/j.mehy.2007.04.052.

[97] Burhani, Mansoor D., and Mark M. Rasenick. "Fish Oil and Depression: The Skinny on Fats." *Journal of Integrative Neuroscience*, vol. 16, no. s1, 2017, https://doi.org/10.3233/jin-170072.

[98] "Facts & Statistics: Anxiety and Depression Association of America, ADAA." Facts & Statistics | *Anxiety and Depression Association of America, ADAA*, https://adaa.org/understanding-anxiety/facts-statistics.

[99] Baldwin, James. "Down At The Cross: Letter from a Region in My Mind." *The Fire Next Time*, Vintage International, New York, 1993, p. 99.

Made in the USA
Las Vegas, NV
10 January 2022

40989508R10143